HEAL MY
Broken Heart

LINAE LLOYD

Cover Design by Nick Toves

Introduction

He heals the brokenhearted and binds up their wounds.
Psalm 147:3 (NKJV)

I know what it is to be devastated in life. I lost my father to mental illness when I was three years old. I prayed for him my whole life believing God would set him free. As a child I had to go to the mental hospital to see my dad. There were electric chairs in the halls, it was a terrible place. He said horrible things that no child should hear. It felt like a hopeless situation that left me brokenhearted. I prayed everyday for my Daddy. I learned to love the unlovely, the down and out, and those struggling through this experience. I learned to love my daddy unconditionally. I was there for him until he took his very last breath. I learned so much about unconditional love. I came to the understanding that this was the father God chose for me. I wanted to get the lesson so I would never have to experience that pain again.

I have come through verbal abuse and a lop sided, unjust divorce. I am a survivor of arsenic poisoning. I broke an engagement to a man I loved, leaving a lifestyle of great wealth and comfort to follow Jesus. I have endured the crushing that comes from someone getting your hopes up, promising to help you with your dreams, only to let you down on countless occasions. I have suffered extreme levels of physical pain in need of a joint replacement in my right jaw, with a pinched nerve running down my back. I have also had God touch my body and heal me. I have been treated like a queen when I had money and treated with contempt when I was in financial hardship. I have lived in the top one percent of wealth, lived in the middle class, and lived in extreme desolation. I have seen how money changes people and how they treat others up close and personal. Money truly exposes what's in a person's heart. I know what it means to be torn violently, to be shattered. I know what it means to have your hopes appear to be demolished beyond repair. Through it all I discovered God's love and blessing is with me wherever I go and no one can take it away. I also learned to let go of regret and the things that hurt me. No matter what has come against me, God is for me and He is faithful. No one can stop His blessing from operating in my life. What God has blessed, no one can curse. No matter how much hardship I've endured, regardless of who has wronged me, God's favor and blessing continues to bring me through to fulfill my destiny. Yes, God is really that powerful.

Many are the afflictions of the righteous
but the Lord delivers him out of them all.
Psalm 34:19 (NKJV)

Through it all I learned to hold on to this promise.
God keeps His word.

There are so many people around the world suffering with a broken heart. They are searching for help. I hope as you read this book you will have many 'aha' moments. I sincerely hope you will find someone you can relate to, who understands what you're going through. I hope you will be encouraged, receive loving guidance, and answers to questions that will bring freedom and truth. I hope this book will give you 'the safe place' you need to allow Jesus to heal your broken heart.

I'm eternally grateful for the privilege to share what I've learned with you. It is my earnest prayer that God will heal your broken heart and fulfill His plans for your life. It's my great joy and honor to share the transforming power of the compassion of Christ and the power of God's amazing love with you.

Jesus moved with compassion to heal the brokenhearted.
He never moved to break their heart more.

And when Jesus went out He saw a great multitude;
and He was moved with compassion for them,
and healed their sick.
Matthew 14:14 (NKJV)

4

Jesus was moved with compassion, which is the capacity to feel deep emotions of sympathy and empathy. Compassion literally means that your heart breaks for someone else. True compassion produces action to alleviate another person's suffering. To show love, to show mercy, to be tenderhearted, to act kindly, and to be generous. Another person's suffering becomes your suffering. This is the meaning of true compassion. Jesus moves with this kind of compassion toward us. The compassion of Christ is profoundly powerful.

CHAPTER 1
Are you brokenhearted?

He heals the brokenhearted and binds up their wounds.
Psalm 147:3 (NKJV)

Let's start by finding out if you're brokenhearted. The definition of brokenhearted in the Hebrew language helps us gain deeper understanding. Hebrew is the original language of the Bible. In Hebrew brokenhearted means: to be broken in pieces, to be torn violently, smashed, broke down, tore down, to be shattered. It means demolished, destroyed, crushed, hurt; something damaged beyond the hope of repair, where nothing can be done. Trauma often leads to a broken heart.

Jesus was damaged beyond the hope of repair on the cross. It looked like all hope was gone. He was torn violently, beaten, bruised, tortured, and crucified. His death left His followers and loved ones heart broken. Three days later Jesus walked out of the grave proving His claims to be the Son of the Living God. He walked out with resurrection power and glory. Jesus triumphed over death, hell, and the grave. Jesus is the hope of the world. He understands what it means to be brokenhearted. He endured the most extreme trauma.

Jesus heals those who are broken in pieces, torn violently, shattered, demolished, destroyed, crushed, and hurt. He heals those damaged beyond the hope of repair, where nothing can be done. He binds up their wounds means: He binds up hurt, gives relief, to bind up a wound; comforting the distressed, bandage, gird about, healer, wrap about, to stop. It means: repairing fortunes to people. Jesus came to heal our hurt, sorrow, trouble and pain. He came to mend and repair our broken heart, to heal us, and makes us whole.

This gives us a much broader view of how wonderful Jesus is. He is our Savior and so much more. Jesus came to this earth to heal our broken heart. He came to give relief to our pain, to heal those damaged beyond the hope of repair, and restore our lives.

God sent Jesus to the earth to heal our broken heart and bind up our wounds. He came to make something beautiful out of all the pain, sorrow, disappointment, devastation, hopelessness, and crushing in our life. I was so grateful to grab a hold of this truth personally because I had a deep desire to be healed, made completely whole, and to help others who are suffering with a broken heart. There are people all around us who are hurting, who don't know where to turn for help. So often people get hurt to the point they begin to question the goodness of God. They begin to question the existence of God. They begin to question their faith and lose hope. During a time of heart break a person can experience emotions of anger toward God. I've met many people who have experienced this.

Jesus came to heal the brokenhearted. This is really good news when you are devastated, completely hopeless, crushed, shattered, and feel damaged beyond repair. I found myself at this place when I was poisoned with arsenic and had to fight for my life. Years later I found myself at this place after years as a Pastor, believe it or not. I know most people can't imagine that, but it's the truth. I endured financial hardship and suffering I had never experienced. It was like nine years of great tribulation and suffering. I was often reminded of how the apostle Paul suffered for the sake of the Gospel during those years. I heard Joni Lamb say they went through a seven year tribulation period. It got so bad Joni questioned if they had missed God. "If this was what God wanted, it wouldn't be this hard." Hearing their story helped me when it got extremely difficult.

When you're trying to do something good and all hell is breaking loose, it breaks your heart. My hardship began when I went in to ministry. I went through intense suffering and affliction. Satan fights what threatens him. God has never lost a battle and He never will. He will bring us through every trial.

**The people who had the greatest favor in the Bible
faced the greatest trials, extreme trials!**

Before I was afflicted I went astray: but now I keep your word.
Psalm 119:67 (NKJV)

Even though Jesus was God's Son,
He learned obedience from the things he suffered.
Hebrews 5:8 (NIV)

The Bible says Jesus learned obedience through suffering. David said before he was afflicted he went astray. There are invaluable lessons learned in a time of great difficulty and suffering. God brought them through to the other side. God did vindicate them in time. He is faithful. Your trouble won't last forever. God will bring you through.

I personally fought the urge to quit several times because of the hardship. I went from living in the top one percent of wealth to extreme hardship. God carried me through by His grace and sent wonderful friends and loved ones to encourage and support me right on time, every time. There were times the different trials and fires left me feeling brokenhearted. Only God would be able to heal and restore my life.

What about you? Do you have a broken heart? Have you lost someone you love to an untimely death and struggled with the loss? Have you felt that God forgot you? Have you ever thought; "God why don't You love me enough to answer my prayers? Are You up there?" Have you ever felt angry at God over a situation that broke your heart? If you've experienced any of this, I hope this book will provide some answers.

Within these pages I pray you find comfort, help, and someone you can relate to. I hope you have many 'aha' moments that begin your transformation. I hope you encounter the goodness of God and experience His love personally. I pray Jesus will reveal His great and mighty love and compassion to you as His grace and power begin to heal your broken heart and bind up your wounds.

Let me show what I learned about Jesus and the brokenhearted.

The Spirit of the Lord God is upon me,
Because the Lord has anointed and commissioned me
To bring good news to the humble and afflicted;
He has sent me to bind up [the wounds of] the brokenhearted,
To proclaim release [from confinement and condemnation]
to the [physical and spiritual] captives
And freedom to prisoners
Isaiah 61:1 (AMP)

The word brokenhearted in this passage is the exact Hebrew word used for brokenhearted in Psalm 147:3. From this we learn that God sent Jesus to the earth to bring us good news in our time of affliction and to heal our broken heart. Most of us know Jesus came to earth to purchase our salvation. He paid a sin debt we could never pay. Jesus was sent so we could be saved and forgiven. Through faith in Christ we have eternal life. Jesus also came to heal the brokenhearted and bind up our wounds. Jesus is the healer of the brokenhearted.

What is the heart? From the Hebrew perspective we learn that the heart is more than an organ that beats in our chest pumping blood. The heart was viewed as the core of a person's being. The heart is the inner man, mind, will, understanding, soul, knowledge, thinking, reflection, memories, inclinations, resolutions, determination, conscience, heart of moral character, seat of appetites, seat of emotions, passions, and the seat of courage. The heart is therefore the center of everything for a person.

God sent and commissioned Jesus to heal our broken heart.

Prayer:
Heavenly Father I place my heart in your hands. I ask Jesus to heal my broken heart and bind up my wounds. Repair me and make me whole. I ask you to restore my life in Jesus name, amen.

CHAPTER 2
Shattered Dreams

My days are past, My purposes are broken off,
Even the thoughts of my heart. They change the night into day;
'The light is near,' they say, in the face of darkness.
Job 17:11-12 (NKJV)

For I know the thoughts that I think toward you, says the Lord,
thoughts of peace and not of evil, to give you a future and a hope.
Jeremiah 29:11 (NKJV)

As we read the Bible, we read about Job who lost everything. His health was gone, his children died, and he lost his fortunes. Job endured some very harsh friends in the time of his devastation. He questioned God and found out that wasn't the answer. Instead of questioning God in the mist of devastation, we need to focus on His great and mighty love, power, faithfulness, and compassion. Job was greatly humbled. Nothing could defeat Job for long, because God is a God of restoration. God healed Job and restored his fortunes. God gave him back double what he lost, when he prayed for his friends.

There are many things that happen in life that shatter our dreams. Divorce leaves mom, dad, children, and extended family members with shattered dreams, broken hearts, and a load of baggage to deal with. Dreams that are not achieved leave us brokenhearted. I have personally come through both. The death of a parent, the loss of a child, a failed business, difficulty in school, the loss of a friend, abuse, a bad break up, and health issues can leave us feeling broken. Maybe nothing, not one thing turned out the way you had hoped and prayed it would. This can make a person feel shattered, worthless, depressed, and even in a fight with thoughts of suicide. Hopelessness stems from a broken heart. A career decision that didn't work out can leave a person feeling useless. A difficult family conflict left unresolved can leave a person with a broken heart, feeling depressed, and hopeless.

What do you do when nothing in your life turned out the way you hoped it would? It's not easy to get up and try again, to hope again, to trust again. When your trust has been broken, your dreams turned into a nightmare, your business struggled, your finances tanked, all of this simultaneously, it breaks your heart. I went through all of this while enduring severe health battles, in excruciating pain. I felt like I was chained to my body, drained, exhausted, and overwhelmed trying to push through to a brighter day. I found many ways that didn't work, but I kept trying. I felt ripped apart trying to keep others whole. I suffered financially, barely making ends meet for years. This hardly fits with the most popular teaching of our day regarding: "The Blessing Of The Lord," being equated to wealth and riches! I do believe God blesses people with wealth to establish his covenant and build His Kingdom. I also believe there's been a gross overemphasis on material wealth, entertainment, and numbers in the church growth movement. The church should be focused on true repentance, solid biblical teaching, prayer, deliverance, and healing the broken. I do believe God will prosper us when we have obedient hearts. There are limitations as to how much you can help others in the midst of a struggle. As we continue to work hard and press toward our dreams, God will remove the limitations. As we place our trust in God and continue to do good even when bad things are happening, God will bring us through to our destiny.

Many people in the Bible went through years of great hardship, but no one could stop God from bringing them into His purpose. It may not have started out well, but it ended well. God will do the same for you and I. Jesus is the same yesterday, today, and forever. God is far bigger, greater and stronger than anything or anyone.

In the Bible we read about Joseph who went through many years of extreme difficulty. His brothers spoke of killing him, they sold him as a slave. Jealousy is a murdering spirit. It will cause people to seek to destroy another person's life and reputation. Joseph's brothers were jealous of him. He lost everything. He was falsely accused of raping a woman, when he did the right thing and refused to violate his bosses wife. He spent years in prison for a crime he did not commit. He was forgotten by the one person he begged to remember him. He must have had a broken heart during those years. He must have missed his mother and father. He must have missed his brothers. Did Joseph do something terrible that caused all of this? No, but everything that happened to Joseph was part of God's plan.

Joseph had great favor from God wherever he went, even though much of what he went through was very difficult. It must have broken Joseph's heart when he was falsely accused of raping a woman. Joseph was punished for doing the right thing. He did what God would have wanted him to do in that situation. He did not give in to temptation. Even though Joseph ended up in prison, God gave him favor there too. Those who faced the most extreme trials in the Bible also had the greatest favor. It may have started out bad, but Joseph finished well. He ended up with great success. He did not get bitter. He continued to do his best wherever he was. God was with Joseph every step of the way, even when it looked bad, it was working for his good. The scriptures tell us all things work together for our good.

And we know that all things work together for good,
to those who love God, to those called according to His purpose.
Romans 8:28 NKJV

Everything that happens doesn't feel good. Some things feel horrible, but in the end it will turn out for our good, if we continue to trust God.

When you have a broken heart it can be hard to understand how anything good could come out of it. God is always working to bring good out of our past, present, and future. God has a good plan, even when it looks like nothing is working out. Trusting God when we don't understand is very important.

Sometimes our plans don't work out, but God is working things out. He will rearrange our destiny to bring forth His plan for our lives. Keep a good attitude, continue to bless others, and God will move on your behalf. Everything in the natural may look bad, but our God is supernatural. God can cause things to turn around in a split second. One good break can turn your life around. God is able. God can cause the same people that wronged you to turn around and bless you. He did this for the Israelites upon their departure from Egypt. God gave them favor with their enemies.

There was a time when the circumstances I faced were so intense, I began to have anxiety attacks. That was something I had never experienced before. In the Bible we find many accounts of people enduring years of hardship. God gives us a promise followed by a problem, to exercise our faith. We have to trust God to bring us through the problem into the promise. This is the journey!

Joseph's dream turned into what looked like a nightmare. But God brought him through and he did arrive at his dream. It was all a set up. That's hard to see when all hell is breaking loose and you're just trying to do the will of God and help others. We find many accounts of God's people enduring hardship. God would remind me of Joseph, David, and Job. God healed their broken heart, restored their lives, and fulfilled their dreams. He is no respecter of persons, he will heal our broken heart and restore us too, but we have to trust Him.

Have you ever tried to do something good and everything around you turned into a nightmare? That is exactly what happened to Joseph. It takes great courage to keep trusting God when everything you hoped for seems to be lost. God allowed David, Joseph, Abraham, Sarah, Job, and many others to go through impossible circumstances. He is the God of the universe who can bypass every natural law and perform miracles on our behalf.

And the Lord restored Job's losses when he prayed for his friends.
Indeed the Lord gave Job twice as much as he had before.
Job 42:10 (NKJV)

Jobs dreams were shattered, but the Lord restored his fortunes when he prayed for his friends. Keep praying for your friends and do all you can to bless them.

God gave Job double to compensate for his loss and suffering.

CHAPTER 3
Anxiety

Anxiety in the heart of man causes depression,
But a good word makes it glad.
Proverbs 12:25 (NKJV)

The word anxiety means: torn apart which is also the definition of brokenhearted. It also means: distracted, feeling dread. We are told in the Bible to be anxious for nothing. Anxiety in the heart weighs us down and causes depression. Stress and fear cause anxiety. Perfect love drives out fear. Jesus is perfect love.

For God has not given us a spirit of fear,
but of power and of love and of a sound mind.
2 Timothy 1:7 (NKJV)

There is no fear in love; but perfect love casts out fear,
because fear involves torment.
But he who fears has not been made perfect in love.
1 John 4:18 (NKJV)

Fear is a tormenting spirit that did not come from God. When anxiety attacks come, we fight back with the word. We pray and trust God. Fear of the unknown is something many people struggle with. Anxiety does not come from God. Anxiety breaks our focus and impacts our relationships because it affects how we relate to other people. Anxiety drives us to make bad decisions by causing us to move too fast. Have you ever made a permanent decision based on a temporary emotion, only to realize it was a big mistake? Anxiety can rob us in many ways. Anxiety is a thief that robs us of peace, love, and joy.

Anxiety keeps us from doing our best. Anxiety keeps us from feeling our best. God has not given us the spirit of fear.

> *Casting all your cares [all your anxieties, all your worries,*
> *and all your concerns, once and for all] on Him,*
> *for He cares about you [with deepest affection,*
> *and watches over you very carefully].*
> *1 Peter 5:7 (AMP)*

We need to give God our concern list. Give Him all your worries. If you're having anxiety, talk to God and tell him how you're feeling. You can be honest and real with God. He knows it all anyway. Trusting God moment by moment helps us overcome anxiety. The challenge is to speak the opposite of the negative emotions, thoughts, and feelings. Fight back with the word of God. The word is full of power.

Prayer:
Lord forgive me for allowing myself to be overcome by fear and anxiety. I believe You're greater than my feelings and circumstances. Thank You for Your comfort, truth, and strength. Nothing is too hard for You Lord. I submit to You God, resist the devil and he must flee. You said I have power to tread on serpents and scorpions and over all the power of the devil. My faith is in someone greater than me, greater than my circumstances, my faith is in Jesus, He can never fail. I raise the shield of faith in Jesus to stop the flaming arrows of the evil one and drive anxiety and fear out. I'm casting my cares on You because You care about me. Thank You for Your promise to never leave me. I trust You to help me. Thank You for Your promise to bring me through every season. Thank You for giving me peace that passes my human understanding. Thank You for the Holy Spirit within me Who is infinitely greater than the spirit of fear and anxiety. Thank You for perfecting Your love in me and driving anxiety, fear, and torment out. I'm putting my hope in Your promises. I'm thankful that You will never disappoint me. Pour Your love into my heart through the Holy Spirit. I will fight the good fight of faith and trust You. Even what the enemy means for evil, You're turning for my good. God is for me, nothing can stand against me. Thank You for the great and mighty things You're doing right now. I overcome Satan by the blood of the Lamb and the

word of my testimony. Greater is He that is in me than he that is in the world. No weapon formed against me shall prosper. God is on my side. If God be for me, who can be against me? God is with me to deliver me. Your compassions fail not, Great is Your faithfulness. Thank You for solutions. Thank You for provision. Thank You for performing miracles right now. Angels are on assignment to help me, I'm an heir of salvation. Thank you for placing me in the center of Your will. This is the victory that overcomes the world, even our faith. Thank You for fulfilling Your promise to me. I believe I will see Your goodness in my life. Thank You for delivering me from fear, anxiety and dread, I put my trust in Jesus Christ instead, amen.

You will keep him in perfect peace,
Whose mind is stayed on You,
Because he trusts in You.
Isaiah 26:3 (NKJV)

I would have lost heart, unless I had believed
that I would see the goodness of the Lord
In the land of the living.
Psalm 27:13 (NKJV)

We need more of Jesus. We have to keep our eyes on Him to win the battle against anxiety and fear. Look up, our help comes from the Lord.

CHAPTER 4
Why Has God Left Me?

My God, My God, why have You forsaken me?
Why are You so far from helping Me,
And from the words of My groaning?
Psalm 22:1 (NKJV)

David is the only man in the Bible who is called: "a man after God's own heart." He wrote: "My God, why have you forsaken me?" Think about that. The word forsaken means: left, abandoned, deserted, failed, helpless, ignored, neglected, left behind, rejected, despised, and to leave destitute.

"God why have you left me? Why have you abandoned me? God why have you ignored me? Why have you left me behind? Why have you rejected me? Why have you left me destitute? God why didn't you answer my prayer?"

David felt abandoned, forsaken, and forgotten by God. Has the pressure ever been so intense in your life that you said: "God are you up there, did you forget me?" I personally experienced this when I was suffering in extreme heart break. Deep within my heart I believed God was up there, but the circumstances were so crushing, it felt like God had forgotten me. I expressed my emotions to God. "My faith can't fail me, if You don't show up for me, there's nowhere left to go." Have you ever felt this way? God doesn't leave us there. God's word is true. God cannot lie. He will show up for us and bring us through.

During His crucifixion Jesus cried out saying: "My God, My God why have you forsaken me?" He understands what you're going through right now.

I found great comfort in reading these words penned by David.

A Psalm of David.
My God, my God, why have You forsaken me?
Why are You so far from helping me, and from the words of my groaning?
O my God, I call out by day, but You do not answer;
And by night, but I find no rest nor quiet.
But You are holy, O You who are enthroned in [the holy place where] the praises of
Israel [are offered]. In You our fathers trusted [leaned on, relied on, and were
confident]; They trusted and You rescued them. They cried out to You and were
delivered; They trusted in You and were not disappointed or ashamed. But I am
[treated as] a worm [insignificant and powerless] and not a man; I am the scorn of
men and despised by the people. All who see me laugh at me and mock me;
They [insultingly] open their lips, they shake their head, saying,
"He trusted and committed himself to the Lord, let Him save him.
Let Him rescue him, because He delights in him."
Psalm 22(AMP)

Have you ever felt the way David felt? There is great comfort knowing a man after God's own heart, experienced the same emotions we experience. It helps to read this Psalm out loud. You're not alone. This is the Psalm of the cross of Jesus Christ, where He finished the work of mankind's redemption. Jesus cried out at the most intense point of His suffering to the Father in heaven: "My God, My God, why have You forsaken Me?" Jesus felt abandoned, rejected, forgotten, and helpless on the cross.

Jesus was touched with everything that could ever touch us. He has compassion for us. He experienced sorrow, pain, suffering, rejection, betrayal, abuse, false accusations, injustice, excruciating torture, and death on the cross. His heart breaks with ours. Jesus understands our human suffering. He has the power to heal our broken heart, forgive our sin, and to perform miracles.

For we do not have a High Priest who is unable to sympathize and understand our
weaknesses and temptations, but One who has been tempted [knowing exactly how
it feels to be human] in every respect as we are, yet without [committing any] sin.
Therefore let us [with privilege] approach the throne of grace [that is, the throne of

God's gracious favor] with confidence and without fear, so that we may receive mercy
[for our failures] and find [His amazing] grace to help in time of need
[an appropriate blessing, coming just at the right moment].
Hebrews 4:15-16 (AMP)

God is gracious in our time of need. He gives us an appropriate blessing at just the right time. What a promise! Jesus personally experienced our pain, sorrow, and suffering. Nothing anyone did to hurt Jesus could stop His destiny. Everything that happened to Jesus did not feel good, but it did turn for good in the end. Jesus walked out of the grave with resurrection power and glory. The life of Jesus Christ is the ultimate story of tragedy turning to triumph. The Bible is the greatest love story ever told. It's the story of mankind's redemption. It's the story of the God of the universe revealing His grace, love, and miracle working power to humanity.

David cried out to God when he felt deserted by Him. He was in pain, calling to God all day long. He got no answer, not a word. He tossed and turned all night. He felt God had abandoned him. He felt like a good for nothing worm. He was shattered and crushed. People were mocking David, shaking their head saying, "If God loves you, let's see Him show up to help you." People said the same thing to Jesus on the cross. Satan will say the same thing to us. "Where is your God?" Tell him; "you're about to find out." Let him know, God is about to show Himself mighty on your behalf. Jesus Christ can never fail. He triumphs when no one else can. God makes a way where there is none.

Recently I was sharing Psalm 22 with someone who was crushed, broken, and devastated. He responded: "wow, I didn't know that was in the Bible, that's exactly how I feel right now." It helps to know we can be vulnerable and honest with God. It's very encouraging to know that David felt the things we feel. He was chosen by God, but he experienced great trials.

There was a time David felt like a worm, worthless, insignificant, powerless, and despised. If you're having these thoughts and feelings, you are not alone. David was a person who was real, honest, made mistakes, and felt like God had abandoned him. David's natural limitations did not stop the supernatural power of God from working in his life. The people who God used to make the greatest impact are also the ones who experienced maximum brokenness. The crushing they endured produced an anointing in their lives. Most don't want to endure that process. The anointing increases when we are crushed. To produce olive oil the olives must be broken and crushed. Everyone wants the power, but are we willing to pay the personal price? God is a rewarder. He looks at the heart. Run to Him, instead of away from Him. Pour your heart out before the Lord.

David was a man after God's own heart. He ran to God when he made mistakes. David poured out his heart before the Lord. David understood it is better to trust God than man. God is rich in mercy. God is the One who holds our future in His hands. When people are harsh and critical toward us, we need to remember God looks at our heart.

David did not start out as a King. He was not the most likely candidate either. I'm sure most would have never believed he would ever become the King of Israel. David went from being a shepherd boy tending his father's sheep, to a delivery boy taking lunch to his brothers. David's brothers were part of the Israeli Defense Forces while he was tending sheep. Sometimes we long for a position that God is still preparing us for. David longed to be part of Israel's army, but his time had not yet come.

During his years as a shepherd, David had to fight a lion and a bear protecting the sheep. Those experiences gave him great confidence in his ability to take down Goliath. David spent a great deal of time alone when he was tending sheep. During those years he spent time in the presence of God. He developed an intimate relationship with God. God's highest priority is a personal relationship with you and I. David wrote many Psalms during those years. We grow stronger in difficult places. Our greatest trials serve as our greatest teachers. We grow wiser as we come through hardship, not in the absence of it.

We learn more in the valley than on the mountaintop. David's experience tending his father's sheep had prepared him to fight Goliath. While the giant intimidated others, David was confident he could remove him with God's help. The private victory David had experienced had given him great confidence. David shot a stone from his sling shot into Goliath's forehead hitting him right between his eyes. Goliath dropped face down. David picked up Goliath's sword and cut off his head. David was seen as a hero. He had delivered Israel from a threat to their national security and stability.

This is the same man who struggled with thoughts of being forsaken by God. The same man who felt like a defeated worm. He overcame with God's help and eventually ruled and reigned as King. He suffered much and he reigned. Are you getting the picture? David became a tremendous leader, a hero, and a success, but he struggled with some of the same issues that we struggle with. I hope this will encourage you tremendously.

David had very difficult family issues. His father in law tried to kill him. He had to hide in caves, he had some serious health battles. He and Bathsheba's baby died. His son Absalom tried to steal the kingdom from him and died a premature death. He saw much blood shed in battle as a man of war. His own army turned against him and spoke of killing him, just to mention a few of the reasons for David's broken heart.

Many are the afflictions of the righteous:
but the Lord delivers him out of them all.
Psalm 34:19 (NKJV)

If we suffer, we shall also reign with him:
if we deny him, he also will deny us.
2 Timothy 2:12 (NKJV)

For though the righteous fall seven times, they rise again…
Proverbs 24:16 (NIV)

Thomas Edison failed 10,000 times trying to discover electric power generation. Most people would have given up. Many would have considered him a man who failed 10,000 times. Instead of giving up, he said: "I've just found 10,000 ways that won't work."

I have found several ways that don't work too, but I'm not giving up. This book was birthed in deep valleys. David went through many hard things, but he didn't quit. He overcame and fulfilled his purpose.

If you prayed for something and God didn't answer, you might think God doesn't love you. I've seen people get to the point where they don't believe in God anymore. Brokenhearted, the enemy starts to speak lies about the goodness of God. He will tell you God doesn't love you. "If God loves you, He would have answered your prayers. If God loves you, why would He allow you to go through all this sorrow? If God is real, why didn't He show up for you?" We must reject those lies and remember, our suffering won't last forever. God will put us back together and restore our lives. He's working all things for our good and for His glory.

If you're going through devastation, this book is intended to throw you a life line. God helps us get our act together. God reveals His love and grace in the midst of our mess. At our lowest point God's grace is the strongest. When a person is down and crushed, we should show them compassion. Jesus moved with great compassion to heal the brokenhearted. He never moved to break their heart more. To do that causes deeper frustration, sorrow, hopelessness, and despair.

Feelings were never meant to lead our lives or determine our decisions. Feelings were given to embellish our lives, not to direct our course. Being ruled by feelings is like living on a roller coaster, up and down without a sense of stability. When we turn to God for help, our feelings change for the better.

David experienced a broken heart and devastating circumstances, yet he still became the King of Israel. Even though David felt forgotten at times, God did not forget him and He won't forget us either. I remember a time I felt alone. I was under extreme financial pressure, in severe physical pain, facing heart wrenching family issues, and what appeared to be my dreams about to collapse. I soaked my pillow with tears. I would beg God: "please, help me. You promised not to give me more than I can handle. What's my lesson?" To overcome the stress I was feeling, I sang praise and worship songs declaring the greatness of God. He is our Way Maker, He heals our broken heart, and continues to perform miracles everyday!

I began asking God questions. "What do I need to do Lord? I don't want to blame anyone else for where I'm at. What do you want from me? What do I need to change? Am I doing what you want?" I almost quit several times under the pressure. God kept me through it all. He was transforming me. During that time I developed a deep compassion for those suffering, beyond anything I could have imagined. Jesus is the Lord of the Breakthrough. He helped me face extremely hard circumstances one after another. Right when I was going to give up, God would provide a way. He lit up the path. He provided the strength I needed to deal with every situation and bring me through. Many things didn't happen the way I thought they would. God knows what's best for our lives. He will allow changes to realign us with His purpose. Those changes can be extremely hard to endure, but He is faithful and true to His word. He will never abandon us. The biggest problems God's people faced, was also where God performed the greatest miracles. God promised that He will never leave us or forsake us. God will bring us through. He is in the business of restoring lives. God is a rewarder.

For He Himself has said, "I will never leave you nor forsake you."
Hebrews 13:5b (NKJV)

Be strong and of good courage, do not fear nor be afraid of them; for the Lord your
God, He is the One who goes with you.
He will not leave you nor forsake you."
Deuteronomy 31:6 (NKJV)

The place you've faced the greatest difficulty is the birthplace of your destiny, when you allow God to heal your broken heart.

CHAPTER 5
I've Lost Hope

Hope deferred makes the heart sick,
But when desire is fulfilled,
it is a tree of life.
Proverbs 13:12 (AMP)

The word deferred means: delayed, to feel weak, afflicted, ill, weakened, wounded, faint, diseased, sorry, strained, stretched, grieved and sick.

God's delay stretches our faith and patience. The scriptures tell us through faith and patience we inherit the promises of God. When what we hope for is delayed, it can make our heart begin to feel strained, weak, afflicted, and sick. We have to hold on to hope when we feel discouraged.

Such hope [in God's promises] never disappoints us,
because God's love has been abundantly poured out within our hearts through the
Holy Spirit who was given to us.
Romans 5:5 (AMP)

The Lord is near to the brokenhearted
and saves those who are crushed in spirit.
Psalm 34:18 (NASB)

The Lord is near to us in times of brokenness. Our heart can literally become sick from our hopes being crushed. We need to be there to help people when they're hurting, not beat them down. I know what it means to have my hope deferred.

For years I struggled in ministry. I worked eight to twelve hour days with very little salary. Many people were healed, we saw miracles, and helped many people. I kept going because of my love for Jesus and the people. I endured extreme hardship. People would come in and tell me they were going to build a church or get me a building. I would get my hopes up, only to be let me down. All at once everything turned upside down. Everything that could cause stress and pressure in my life occurred at the same time. It was in every direction.

Have you ever felt like everything that could come against a person was coming against you? I understand, I have endured this personally. There were so many struggles during that time, including almost unbearable pain in my body. I felt exhausted, my hopes were completely deferred. I felt like Job. I talked to God about how I felt. "God I believe You're up there, how can You allow this? I don't want to get my hopes up to be crushed one more time. Have I wasted the last 9 years of my life? How can this be where I have arrived? Where did I go wrong? I thought I was doing what you wanted?" Every time things started to turn around, there was another devastating blow. Sometimes we can't understand why God allows different trials, but we have to trust Him.

Our heart can literally become sick when our hopes are crushed. There were years in my life that were so hard, my hopes were deferred. God always lights the way and brings us through. Instead of becoming negative, we have to train ourselves to speak words of life. We have to train ourselves to speak the opposite of the negative emotions we are feeling.

Prayer:
Thank You Lord, You are the hope of the world. Your hope is the anchor to my soul. Hope does not disappoint because Your love is poured into my heart by the Holy Spirit. You are all powerful. You are good and Your mercy endures forever. You are invincible, indestructible, incorruptible, all powerful, God of the impossible. You are faithful and true. You are an awesome provider. It is impossible for You to lie. You are a rewarder of those who diligently seek You. I'm diligently seeking You. Your word does not return to You void. You said no weapon formed against me will prosper. When the enemy comes in, like a flood You raise a standard against him. Your blessing is upon Your people. You said you can't curse what God has blessed, I am blessed. Thank You for giving

me success. Thank You for opening doors for me that no one can close and closing doors no one can open. Thank You for giving me the desires of my heart that are according to Your will. I'm the head and not the tail, above and not beneath. Thank You for causing me to prosper and be in health. Thank You for causing my soul to prosper. Thank You for sending Your word to heal me and deliver me from all my destructions. Thank You for restoring everything that has been stolen and bringing me out with plenty. Thank You for contending with those who contend with me, for fighting against those who fight against me. It's not by might or power, but by Your Spirit. I can do all things through Christ, He is strengthening me. The Spirit of the Lord is upon me, because You have anointed me. I still believe this is true. You are greater than my mistakes and everyone else's. All things are possible. You are limitless. Thank You for all that I have. Thank You for my family and all the wonderful people in my life. Thank You for the people I've had the privilege to help. Thank You for ordering my steps. Thank You for going before me, circling around me and bringing up my rear guard. You're the God of all flesh, nothing is too hard for You. Thank You for all the miracles You're performing right now. Thank You for the privilege to know You. Thank You for making something beautiful out of all the broken places in my life. Thank You for Your amazing love. Thank You for showing Yourself strong and mighty in every situation. Great is Your faithfulness. I know Your plans for my life are good. Accomplish Your will in my life. Thank You for angels with great power and authority that are here to assist me. Thank You for leading me to the promised land that You have ordained for my life. Thank You for everything You've brought me through. Thank You for always showing me Your faithfulness, provision, blessings, and love. Thank You for revealing Jesus to me. Thank You for being with me every step of the way. Thank You for making a way where I don't see one. I love You Lord in Jesus name, amen.

When there is no human way possible, God will make a way!

CHAPTER 6

When There Is No Human Reason Left For Hope

[For Abraham, human reason for] hope being gone,
hoped in faith that he should become the father of many nations,
as he had been promised,
So [numberless] shall your descendants be.
Romans 4:18-22 (AMPC)

Abraham is called the Father of faith, but he made mistakes along the way. After waiting many years, he and Sarah tried to make the dream God gave them come true. They got another woman involved named Hagar. This decision caused great heartache. Abraham also lied about Sarah being his wife due to fear and the desire for self preservation. He gave Sarah to another man in Egypt. I sure wouldn't appreciate my husband giving me away to a strange man in a foreign country. God intervened to save Sarah and restore her to her husband. These historical accounts are recorded to encourage us. They were people who made mistakes. They were ordinary people like you and I, who trusted in an extraordinary God. It took 25 years before Abraham and Sarah saw the realization of the promise God made to them. By the time their dream came true, it was humanly impossible. I hope this encourages you. You are not too far gone. You are not too old, you did not miss your moment. God is faithful. He loves you.

There was no human hope left for the promise God gave Abraham regarding having a son with Sarah. She had been barren for years and was past menopause. Abraham's body wasn't functioning in the same capacity anymore either. The Bible says his body was as good as dead. They were old. All human hope was gone.

And not being weak in faith, he did not consider his own body,
already dead (since he was about a hundred years old),
and the deadness of Sarah's womb.
Romans 4:19 (NKJV)

It's when there is absolutely no human way possible, that the God of the impossible performs His word. Our impossibility is truly God's specialty. He allows our circumstances to get to the point where He alone will get the glory. I learned personally what Abraham meant by hoping against hope during my times of great difficulty and brokenness. When everything looked completely hopeless and all human effort had failed, God showed Himself faithful and true. He is the God of the impossible. God allows things to get to the point where you will know beyond a shadow of a doubt it was Him.

I was told we are never to let anyone know what we're going through in ministry. Never let them see you sweat. The Bible records human struggles, broken hearts, and impossible circumstances. It also reveals how God intervened and performed miracles on behalf of His people. I truly believe the closer we are to Jesus the more transparent, humble, and honest we will be. When we have nothing to hide, there is freedom. Tell on yourself and strip the devil of his power to blackmail you. Our life is meant to be an open book for others to read. We are living letters. The Bible gives us historical accounts of people who had character flaws. Real people who made mistakes, endured hardship, and struggles. They could not have gotten to their destiny without God's divine intervention. The scriptures are filled with stories of people who learned to trust God through difficult times and hardship. Stories of people with broken hearts that God healed. People with shattered dreams that God restored. God brought them through it all. He didn't leave them. The Bible is a love letter written to you and I. There is an acronym for Bible: "Basic Instructions Before Leaving Earth." If what you are going through right now is humanly impossible, remember all things are possible with God. He stills performs miracles everyday. Put your hope in the Lord.

Be of good courage, And He shall strengthen your heart,
All you who hope in the Lord.
Psalm 31:24 (NKJV)

Jesus Is The Hope Of The World

CHAPTER 7
Depression

Let's look at Elijah's struggle with depression.

But he himself went a day's journey into the wilderness,
and came and sat down under a broom tree.
And he prayed that he might die, and said,
"It is enough! Now, Lord, take my life,
for I am no better than my fathers!"
1 Kings 19:4 (NKJV)

Have you ever been hurting so badly, felt so hopeless that you prayed you would die? Have you ever said, "Lord take my life?" Most of the people I have asked this question answered yes. You are not alone. God promised not to give us more than we can handle. He is not a man that He should lie. When we are at our wits end, God will come through. He makes a way where there is none.

When Jezebel threatened Elijah's life, he prayed that he would die. He asked God to kill him. Elijah had just won a tremendous victory. From this account we see how a perceived threat to our life can lead to deep despair. It also teaches us how the Jezebel spirit comes against a prophet of the Living God. Elijah experienced depression, however Elijah did not stay in that place. God brought him through and He will bring you through too.

There are many things that can lead to depression. Severe trauma, chronic pain, and serious health issues can cause to depression. When a person feels rejected by parents, friends, or other people, they can begin to feel depressed. A person can feel hopeless when nothing they do brings the acceptance and love they desire. This happens in marriages, families, friendships, churches and social clubs.

As long as we're alive, we will both want and need the approval of our parents. Sometimes we have to turn to God for that approval because our parents were incapable of giving us that love and acceptance. If a parent is always harsh, critical, and demeaning a person will feel that nothing they do will ever be good enough. If a parent never expresses words of exhortation and love, a child will have an empty love cup. Parents have the power to speak words that bring healing to their children, regardless of their age. It's important to speak words of love and encouragement. The words I love you, I'm proud of you, and I believe in you carry power to bring healing to your child's broken heart. Words are very powerful for good and for evil.

Grown children must understand that a person cannot give you something they don't have. Your parent may have been so broken, they were never able to give you the affirmation you needed. Parents are often brokenhearted too. The way a person treats their children is a reflection of what's going on in their heart. The parent who is unable to express love to their own child is usually suffering from a broken heart. It's the old saying: "hurting people, hurt people," it's true.

God holds parents accountable for how they threat their children. The scriptures expressly tell parents they are not to provoke their children to anger. God will hold us accountable for how we treat our children. If you have failed in this area, repent. Leave the old pattern, don't repeat it again. Create a new pattern. Make a conscience decision to grow in love.

People who were raised with verbal abuse have to make a conscience decision they're not going to repeat the pattern. When disciplining your child, if you feel anger rising up, go outside and count to ten or twenty. Discipline your child from a place of calm, it's a choice you have to make. Take the good things you received from your parents and throw out the negative patterns. You can stop the negative cycle. Refuse to repeat the patterns that hurt you the most.

I've heard parents say: "I love my child, but I don't like them." This is especially prevalent during the teen years when a child has decided they know everything. When a teenager is strong willed and rebellious they can cause the parent to suffer with anxiety and depression. When a teenager is being manipulative and critical of their parent, the parent can get depressed. This goes both ways. The parent is supposed to be the grown up in the situation, but parents are imperfect people. If someone is under your roof, they are under your rules. Three simple things can solve a lot of problems.

1. You can't hurt yourself
2. You can't hurt someone else
3. You can't hurt things
It's simple, but it covers a lot of ground.

Both David and Elijah battled depression. Elijah asked God to kill him. Depression and thoughts of suicide can enter a person's mind when they have a broken heart or when a persons life and security is threatened. If you're depressed you may need to seek medical help. It's possible your brain is not producing the chemicals it needs.

I recently heard about a Pastor that committed suicide. In his depression, he felt he had no where to turn. As a believer we need to make sure we help others come out of depression in every way we can. We must reach out with hearts of compassion, never pushing someone further down into darkness and hopelessness.

Several years ago my path crossed with a homeless man on the street who was down and out. I smiled at him and said: "hello." I spoke some encouraging words, said a prayer with him, and went on my way. I saw him several months later at a church gathering I was attending. He said: "I wanted to say thank you. Things are going really well. Everything you said happened. I got a job and a place to live, things have turned around." I was so happy to hear his good report. A smile, words of encouragement, and a prayer can impact someone's life. To God be all the glory.

A threat to your life can lead to depression. A threat to your stability can lead to depression. Focusing on negativity can cause depression. Broken dreams can lead to depression. Comparing yourself to others can cause depression. The list goes and on and on. I truly believe focusing our thoughts on the goodness of God and being thankful is a natural remedy for depression.

The Apostle Paul said to send relief so he didn't have to take up a special offering for those in the church who were suffering. What has happened to us when we have no compassion for those who are suffering among us? Many people put money toward a building, but ignore those suffering among them. Compassion is love in action.

Therefore, to him who knows to do good
and does not do it, to him it is sin.
James 4:17 ((NKJV)

Elijah asked God to kill him after Jezebel threatened his life. He sat under the broom tree distressed, having lost all hope. Elijah, the great prophet of God prayed for death. God sent an angel to strengthen Elijah and told him to get up. God had more for Elijah to accomplish. God strengthened Elijah to continue and brought him out of depression. He will do the same for you and I. Jezebel hates God's people, especially an anointed prophet of God. In the end Elijah came out victorious and Jezebel died a terrible death. God turned the tables completely. God is so much more powerful than any enemy that comes against us. No one can stop God's plan for our lives. We must continue to seek His will and never give up.

When a person feels hopeless, they can ask God to take them out. You may be thinking what you're going through is too much. Maybe you don't have the stability or security you feel you need. I recently had someone tell me: "I wish the Lord would take me home." The physical pain they were in left them feeling hopeless. If you've ever had these thoughts, remember God can turn the tables completely. God is for you. He will never leave you or forsake you. In difficult times, God remains our hope. He is the same yesterday, today, and forever. No matter how dark things get, light rises in the midst of darkness for the godly. God is our hope for a brighter day.

Remember your word to your servant, for you have given me hope.
Psalm 119:49 (NIV)

Our feelings are not the best barometer to live by. Our feelings change, but God remains the same forever. God did not intend for us to live out of our emotions. God gave us emotions to embellish our lives, not to direct our decisions.

David wrote this Psalm:

Why are you cast down, O my soul?
And why are you disquieted within me? Hope in God; For I shall yet praise Him,
The help of my countenance and my God.
Psalm 42:11 (NKJV)

Our self talk impacts our future. We need to cheer ourselves on when we're going through a difficult season. Speak this Psalm over yourself. Thoughts have a presence. Our thoughts, words, and actions impact our success and future blessings. When we have faith, hope, and love in our heart, we gain the power necessary to overcome.

There will come a time in your life when you'll have to encourage yourself. I call it "The Dark Night Of The Soul." There will be a time in your life when no one else is available to encourage you. This is a place intended for us to grow in our personal relationship with the Lord. It's meant to build our faith and develop our character. Instead of running to God like David, many people run to the world, drugs, alcohol, and other things to deal with difficulty. This leads to more problems. Make the choice to run to God.

When we make the decision to encourage ourselves with the word, we get to see God's love and power work on our behalf. It's amazing and humbling when God shows up to bring us out of darkness into His glorious light. When dreams are fulfilled, it is a tree of life. God wins every battle. He can never lose. Jesus triumphs when absolutely no one else can. On the other side of the difficult circumstances is an experiential anointing. We grow in wisdom and gain strength to overcome and help others. We get to see the goodness of God personally.

David had to encourage himself and so do we. Our soul is our mind, will, and emotions. Our self talk is important. Make the decision to tell your mind, will, and emotions to hope in God. Speak words of life and victory.

Prayer:
Heavenly Father I praise You. I set my will to trust You. Thank You for helping me get my lesson so I can move forward. Thank You for helping me fix my mind on You. Give me a heart that is steadfast and loyal to You. Thank You for filling me with expectancy. Thank You for supernatural breakthrough. Things are turning in my favor. Thank You Lord for victory. Thank You for breaking every stronghold in my life. Your joy gives me strength. Thank You for divine protection, divine provision, supernatural power, divine healing, and divine connections. Thank You for angelic and human help. Thank You for blessing me to be a blessing. Thank You for perfecting, establishing, strengthening, and settling me. Thank You for beginning a good work in me, You will perform it until the day of Jesus Christ. I'm grateful Your word never returns void, Your word accomplishes all it was sent to do. Thank You for transforming my life. Thank You for helping me occupy until You come. Thank You Jesus, You are The Lord of the Breakthrough, amen.

When David was down in the dumps, his self talk shifted from defeat to speaking the promises of God. He spoke God's word to his soul. He told himself to hope in God. He told himself that His God will help him and give him a reason to smile again. There is always hope when you trust God. King David went through what many of us experience in a place of brokenness.

The sacrifices of God are a broken spirit,
A broken and a contrite heart—
These, O God, You will not despise.
Psalm 51:17 (NKJV)

A person with a broken spirit is broken in pieces. A broken and contrite heart means: crushed, in physical distress, to collapse physically or mentally, to break.

A person with a broken and contrite heart is a someone with godly sorrow for the things they've done. It's a place of humility. God gives grace to the humble.

People around you may despise you when you're crushed, but God will not. No matter who has rejected you, God loves you. God is for you. God is on your side. God wants you to run to Him for help.

CHAPTER 8
Artificial Life Support - God Is The Source Of All Life

The scriptures tell us that Jesus is the source of life.

In the beginning was the Word, and the Word was with God, and the Word was God. He was in the beginning with God. All things were made through Him, and without Him nothing was made that was made.
In Him was life, and the life was the light of men.
John 1:1-4 (NKJV)

God is the source of all life. When we don't go to the source of life for healing, we will turn to artificial life support. This includes drugs, alcohol, sex, eating disorders, shopping addictions, social media, video gaming, pornography, the list goes on and on.

Some people go to rehab again and again in an effort to break free from their addiction. When there are failed attempts to break an addiction the root issue is a broken heart. There is a stronghold that must be broken.

To feel emotions is something we all experience because we're alive. When we've been devastated and we don't deal with the issues behind our broken heart, we will run to artificial forms of life support to numb the pain. Life can be hard. Artificial life support is often used as a means of coping with difficulty. People are looking for an alternative reality as a means of escape. People are self medicating to numb the pain in their heart. This doesn't heal anyone and does more damage. The truth is the conflict we won't face can never be erased. The time comes when we must decide we want to get real and be honest with ourselves. You cannot medicate away a broken heart. You cannot buy enough to heal a broken heart. You cannot get high enough to heal a broken heart. God is the healer of broken hearts. Run to Him and give Him your heart. He longs to heal you and give you a success story. God takes the worst tragedy and turns it into triumph.

I've known people with great wealth, people in the upper and lower middle class, and those living in poverty who were self medicating. They were all trying to numb the pain in their heart. Money solves many problems, but it can't heal a broken heart.

When glass is broken and we pick it up with our hands, we get cut. So it is with the broken life. God is a Master Designer. When we allow God to pick up the broken pieces of our lives, He creates a master piece. Mosaic art made from shattered glass is often spectacular in beauty. Special instruments are used to pick up each piece of shattered glass. Broken glass is fragile and razor sharp. If we pick the glass up with our bare hands, we'll get cut and bleed. How many of us have been hurt more attempting to fix our broken lives instead of allowing God to heal us?

Allow God to have all the pieces of your broken heart and ask Him to make a masterpiece. Mosaic art can be breathtakingly beautiful. The shattered pieces of glass create a magnificent work of art where nothing is wasted. There would be no mosaic art without broken pieces of glass. Jesus has the power to pick up all the pieces of our broken heart, put us back together, and make our life a radiant masterpiece.

In church we hear the message of salvation, however Jesus came to do more than save us. He came to bind up our wounds, and heal our broken heart. Jesus came to set us free. I truly believe this message is crucial for the church. There are as many people who are brokenhearted in churches as there are in the world. Many people have spent years in church, but they're still broken. There are people who are desperate for help. Some have been lost along the way. We need to help the brokenhearted to heal instead of hurting them more.

CHAPTER 9
I'm Afraid To Tell Anyone My Struggle

The fear of man brings a snare,
But whoever trusts in the Lord shall be safe.
Proverbs 29:25 (NKJV)

Fear is a dangerous trap.
It paralyzes, restricts, and blocks our freedom.

David talked about the pain of loneliness. He didn't cover up his struggles or hide his feelings. David expressed himself to God when he felt weak. When David felt like a failure, was troubled or lonely; he cried out to the Lord even more. No one is called to walk in this life alone. Isolation can be devastating. Disconnection can lead to great peril. Satan works hard to isolate people. God connects us for His purpose and to enrich our lives. We need each other.

Many people are afraid to tell anyone their struggle. Some people are too ashamed to tell anyone what they've been through. They fear they will face more abuse, hurt, and rejection if they're honest.

True love is demonstrated when compassion and actions meet.

I had a man come to me who shared the trauma he experienced as a child. He was sexually abused by a man. He told me this caused confusion regarding his sexual identity, but he knew he was attracted to women. He hadn't been able to tell anyone because of fear and shame. He had hidden this area of his life in darkness, afraid of being rejected. He became an alcoholic and was using drugs to numb his pain. He was vexed by demons who tormented him about the abuse, until he brought it into the light. He struggled to forgive the man. I suggested instead of rehearsing the trauma, when those thoughts come to your mind, start a process of forgiveness. Every time he comes to your mind, say: "I forgive him through faith in Christ and make Jesus Lord over the gross feelings." At first it was hard for him, he didn't feel any different. As he continued to make that choice, he started overcoming the darkness. It didn't happen overnight. It was a process. He felt anger toward God for allowing the abuse in his life. He decided to let go of the anger and ask Jesus to come into every part of his heart. He asked God to heal and deliver him. Eventually he was able to overcome the addictions, receive healing, and deliverance. He is happily married with children.

Everyone needs a safe place to share their struggle. God wants us to be a safe place for those hurting and broken. We should strive to help bring reconciliation and restoration.

David talked to God about his problems. God wants you to turn to Him. You may have been stuck for a while, but God can help you shift gears and overcome the problems that have held you back.

When others are suffering, we need to throw them a life line. Jesus has a heart full of compassion and mercy to bring healing to the brokenhearted. People need the love and compassion of Jesus.

A woman who came out of a life of prostitution was driven out of a large church. She still wore skin tight clothing, therefore she was rejected. This is very sad. People need time to grow and develop. They need a safe place where their broken heart can be healed, not broken more. They need a place where they can be restored. We need to provide people with a safe place where the love of God can heal them.

A few young people recently told me they're battling depression, anger, and rejection because of their parents divorce. They were devastated by the way their parents spoke to them. They're crushed by the division between their mom and dad. They are hurt because of what they're going through with their friends. Verbal abuse is the root of many who are suffering with a broken heart. For others it's physical and sexual abuse. Many young people are in need of the healing only Jesus brings to a broken heart.

The scriptures say a lot about words. God's word is life and health to all our flesh. Death and life are in the power of the tongue. Our battle is to speak words of life, not words of death and defeat. Our words impact everything and everyone around us. If you haven't found someone to share your heart with, open the book of Psalms and read them out loud. It's a great way to learn to express yourself to God.

CHAPTER 10

I'm Never Going
To Be Good Enough
So Why Even Try

[Not in your own strength] for it is God Who is all the while
effectually at work in you [energizing and creating in you the power and desire],
both to will and to work for His good pleasure
and satisfaction and delight
Philippians 2:13 (AMPC)

I recently had a young man tell me, "I could never live up to God's standard, why even try?" The Bible teaches us that it's not going to be in our own strength. It's not by might or human power, it's by the power of the Holy Spirit. It's not in our own strength, it is God Who is all the while effectually at work in us. He is the One energizing and creating in us the power and desire, both to will and to work for His good pleasure, satisfaction, and delight.

God's grace empowers us to do what we were unable to do without Him. All have sinned and fallen short. Everyone has broken God's moral law. We all need the power of God in our lives to overcome the world, the flesh, and the devil. We have the cross, the blood of Jesus, and the resurrection power of the Holy Spirit. He gave us the word, angel armies, and people to encourage us and help us accomplish His will. What we can't do without Christ, we can do with Him. God takes us as His own.

I can do all things through Christ who strengthens me
Philippians 4:13 (NKJV)

Although my father and my mother have abandoned me,
Yet the Lord will take me up [adopt me as His child].
Psalm 27:10 (AMP)

I mentioned in a previous chapter the devastation that can occur if one or both of our parents were hard on us. When a parent is critical all the time, a person will feel that nothing they do will ever be good enough. Some parents are extremely hard on their children. A child needs ten words of encouragement for every criticism. Our job as a parent is to build our children up, not tear them down. Abuse can come in many different forms from a parent. Rejection, verbal abuse, physical abuse, and sexual abuse. Ignoring a child, withholding the encouragement and love they need is very destructive. All of this breaks a child's spirit and can lead to patterns of depression, rebellion, self sabotage, anxiety disorders, promiscuity, alcoholism, drug addiction, and many other serious struggles.

Everyone wants the love and approval of their parents. When your mother or father abused you, it impacts you deep in your heart. Our father and mother are the pillars of our self image when we're children. When one or both of those pillars is knocked down, a dangerous vacuum is created. God is the One who can fill that void in our heart. When we don't turn to the source of life, a person will try to fill that vacuum with something else. People start looking for love in all the wrong places and end up with more heart ache.

When the people who were supposed to love and protect us break our heart, we can struggle with authority figures. This can make it more challenging to trust God. When you meet people who grew up with wonderful, loving parents they seem to naturally trust in the goodness of God. When you meet people who were hurt and abused by one or both parents, there is often a struggle to trust God. God is good regardless of who hurt us or let us down.

When you don't feel good enough for your parents and you never measured up to that critical spouse, you can feel like you'll never be good enough. When you failed at something you gave your best effort, you can struggle with feelings of never measuring up.

What do you do when it seems like God is rejecting you? If I'm not good enough for God, I will never be good enough for anyone. Have you ever had that thought? It seems David had that thought at times, yet God was with David in a mighty way. No matter what it looks like right now, God has not forgotten you. Sometimes God allows extremely difficult circumstances, but in time we discover that His grace is what carried us through. God uses adversity to develop our character and teach us invaluable lessons. There comes a time when we have believe that God is for us and leave our past behind. As we trust and obey God, He will take up our case. God holds the universe together, why not trust Him to heal your broken heart? Place your life and times in God's hands. God longs to reveal His love, goodness, and kindness to you.

God will take you as you are, but he doesn't leave you there. Jesus is the ultimate Superhero. He has the power to help you overcome thoughts of self defeat.

Prayer:
Thank You Heavenly Father, though it seemed like I wasn't good enough for You, I'm grateful You see me through the perfection of Jesus. Thank You Jesus for freeing me from a life of sin, death, depression, failure, pain, rejection and brokenness. Thank You for taking me as Your own in Jesus name, amen.

If your mother and father reject you, God will still love you. God will not forget you. Ask God to help you overcome negative, destructive patterns and feelings of never being good enough. Jesus was a fisher of men. When you catch a fish, it's not instantly cleaned up. No one comes to the Lord clean, we have all sinned and fallen short. If people had to be clean before they came to Jesus, no one would ever be saved.

Jesus came to seek and to save you. You are more precious to God than all the silver and gold in the world. His love for you is great and mighty. Jesus loved you enough to suffer beyond what you can imagine to save you, to destroy the power of the devil in your life, and to heal your broken heart.

No matter what your feelings are telling you,
God loves you and longs to heal you.

"Can a woman forget her nursing child,
And not have compassion on the son of her womb?
Surely they may forget, Yet I will not forget you.
Isaiah 49:15 (NKJV)

To the praise of the glory of His grace,
by which He made us accepted in the Beloved.
Ephesians 1:6 (NKJV)

No one can be as hard on us, as we can be on ourselves. Don't be so hard on yourself. No one is perfect but Jesus. Give yourself a break! Love believes the best and that includes believing the best about you. I encourage you to place your life in God's hand and see what He will do. Jesus is the One Who will heal your broken heart and bind up your wounds. Jesus Christ has to power to heal and restore your life. He is really that amazing and powerful.

CHAPTER 11
If I Don't Fit In At Church Where Do I Go?

And let us consider one another in order to stir up love and good works, not
forsaking the assembling of ourselves together,
as is the manner of some, but exhorting one another,
and so much the more as you see the Day approaching.
Hebrews 10:24-25 (NKJV)

Don't give up because you didn't fit it in somewhere along the way. We need each other. God could put someone in your life today that causes everything to fall into place. There are many wonderful churches who are doing a great work for the Lord and helping hurting people. No church is perfect. Many are not equipped to handle severe issues people are experiencing. Sometimes the best they can do is direct you to those who are equipped to help you.

As I was writing this book I heard many stories of people who went to church searching for help and got hurt even more. There are people who have an elitist mentality. Some people will look down their nose in an attitude of superiority, snobbery, and judgement rather than love, mercy, and compassion. In that case move on, but refuse to be offended. We are supposed to die in Christ and become a new creation. When we are truly dead to self, we don't carry offense anymore. It's not about me, it's about Jesus. Let it go and move on.

Judging others in their time of suffering does more harm than good.
We should strive to be more like Jesus than Job's friends.

There is a vast difference between a person under the influence of a religious spirit and a person filled with the Holy Spirit. A few years ago I spoke with a wonderful christian friend mourning the devastating loss of her daughter. People with a religious spirit were critical, harsh, and judgmental. They said things that were completely inappropriate during a time of grief, adding more sorrow. A religious spirit is what fueled the people who hated Jesus. Satan is a religious devil. A person with the Spirit of Christ displays love, compassion, and comfort in our time of suffering. The heart of Jesus is one of compassion. When a person's heart is filled with the Holy Spirit they will move with compassion to alleviate another person's suffering.

No one cares how much you know,
until they know how much you truly care.

The Pharisees never cared about those who were hurting. They cared about outward appearances. They cared about sitting in the best seat in the synagogue, looking important. They were proud, unteachable, cold, and selfish. They had head knowledge but lacked true love and compassion. They saw themselves above others. They desired power and control over others. They were wealthy, wore expensive clothing and had fancy buildings, but they lacked love and compassion for people. They were always trying to catch Jesus in a word trap so they could bring accusations against Him. Satan is the accuser of the brethren. They observed Jesus with a critical eye, always looking for fault. They were hell bent on finding something wrong, which caused them to miss out on what was right. They missed out on God's greatest gift and blessing for their own life. The Pharisees were not big enough to stop the plans of Almighty God. No one is powerful enough to stop the plans of the God of the universe in your life. That is good news!

There are many people today that act like the Pharisees. They hide behind a mask attempting to conceal the motives of their heart. They do more harm than good to those who are suffering. They focus on outward appearances, but Jesus said inside they were dead mens bones. He called them a brood of vipers. They love money and power more than God. They live in serious compromise and hold themselves to a different standard than others. They are cold, judgmental, and arrogant. They will get your hopes up, to let you down. They use their power and money to control and manipulate others. Instead of looking for ways to serve and bless others, their focus is always: "what's in it for me?" They have a selfish agenda. Their heart is not right within them.

Love is not selfish.

A person filled with the Holy Spirit will do whatever they can to alleviate another persons suffering, expecting NOTHING in return. They give as unto the Lord. They look for ways to be a blessing to others. They express love, kindness, generosity, humility, and a heart of true compassion. Compassion is immensely powerful. It is propelled by true love.

True compassion produces action to alleviate another person's suffering, not to increase it. The good news is the Pharisees were not big enough to stop the God of all flesh. Your critics cannot stop you from arriving at your destiny. Keep pressing on and let God deal with your critics.

When God wants to bless you, He sends a person.
When Satan wants to destroy you, He copies God.
Your job is to know the difference.

Hearing God's words of love and encouragement spoken over your life is powerful. God's word is creative power that can lift you up and transform your life.

Speak words of love and encouragement
instead of words of criticism and defeat.

Refuse to allow the bad things that have happened to you to make you become negative. The enemy will try to get you to expect bad things to continue to happen. Say no to that! No matter what happens to you, keep doing the right thing. Keep honoring God and being generous and kind to others. God will bring you through to a new day. God is a rewarder.

Therefore, as God's chosen people, holy and dearly loved, clothe yourselves with
compassion, kindness, humility, gentleness and patience.
Colossians 3:12 (NIV)

For the Son of Man has come to seek and to save that which was lost.
Luke 19:10 (NKJV)

If you feel like you're lost right now, Jesus is seeking to save you. You are the reason He came to the earth. Jesus said that when one sheep is lost, He would leave the ninety-nine to look for the one who has strayed. Jesus loves you.
Many people have shared their struggle to find a church where they feel a sense of belonging. They don't feel they can ever measure up or fit in anywhere. I encourage everyone to keep looking and pray. Ask God to lead you to your spiritual family, they are out there somewhere. There are some wonderful home meetings as well.

One young teenager told me she was rejected more from christians than any other people. She told me that she didn't believe in God anymore because of how much she had been hurt in church and christian schools. Christians are just people who make mistakes. Refuse to allow the negative things people have done to you, to rob you of your faith. Refuse to allow the people who didn't love you, to keep you from finding the ones who will.

Instead of expecting more disappointment, start expecting to see the goodness of God. Believe God for something new and wonderful to happen. Believe you will find a church or a group of people that is perfect for you. Ask God to amaze you. The God who governs the universe is able to connect you to the right people. Ask God to lead you to His perfect will. God sets the lonely in families. He will help you find your tribe.

Prayer:
Heavenly Father I thank You for Who You are. I thank You for all You've brought me through. Thank You for the power of Your love. Thank You for helping me find my tribe, Thank You for leading me to my spiritual family, I expect to see Your goodness and blessings in my life. I'm letting go of everything behind me. Thank You for opening doors for me and changing

wrong attitudes within me. Thank You for changing people's attitude toward me. Root and ground me in Your love so I can show Your love to others. I will be strong in You Lord and the power of Your might. Thank You for Your watchful eyes that are on me. Thank You for hearing my prayers. Thank You for providing all my needs according to Your riches in glory in Christ Jesus. Thank You for giving me faith to soar to heights I've never seen. Thank You for leading me to the right place, at the right time. Thank You for connecting me with the people You have ordained for my destiny. Thank You for watching over my steps and protecting me. Thank You for Your favor and blessing upon my life and family. Thank You Lord that You qualify the unqualified. I bless and honor You. Thank You for Your faithfulness. Be it unto me as You have spoken in Jesus name, amen.

> *Blessed be the God and Father of our Lord Jesus Christ,*
> *the Father of mercies and God of all comfort,*
> *who comforts us in all our tribulation,*
> *that we may be able to comfort those who are in any trouble,*
> *with the comfort with which we ourselves are comforted by God.*
> *2 Corinthians 1:3-4 (NKJV)*

When everything is going great people will love you. When a person is broken, crushed, and struggling people are often harsh critics. People with a religious spirit are critical observers. The Holy Spirit moves in compassion, love, and kindness. God doesn't want us to have an attitude of self righteousness or a sense of superiority. We are called to restore others in a spirit of gentleness, grace, and humility.

Warning: Be careful how you treat those who are crushed, hurting, and broken because in the future it could happen to you.

I am not talking about enabling manipulative, destructive, abusive or toxic behavior. I am talking about helping those who are seeking help. Helping those who are stuck. Throwing a life line to those who are drowning. Giving them love and encouragement. If we are not equipped to help them, we should do our best to point them in the direction where they can get the help they need.

True compassion produces action
to alleviate another persons suffering

The scripture says your gift will make a way for you. God can and will open doors of destiny. He will bring forth divine connections making a way for a bright future. God knows how to get us right where we need to be. Even if you can't see a way in sight, God has one. Everything we come through becomes a testimony of the faithfulness of God. God will help us get to the other side with a heart that has been revived.

God is able to cause opportunities to find us. God has divine connections set up for us. When we continue to do God's will, He will send the right people into our life. Things can shift in our favor suddenly. God will not leave us in our struggle. He will open doors of opportunity for us. God will direct our course, leading us to the promised land. God can cause the people who were against us, to change their mind. There is no limit to God's power. He is the God of all flesh. God can move in your midst, aligning a breakthrough that takes you from barely getting by, to the land of more than enough. He did it for me, He will do it for you. God is no respecter of persons. God respects faith. God can bring you out of any pit and place your feet in the palace in on day. God can bring your dreams to pass suddenly. We serve a mighty God who controls the universe. He is all powerful.

The compassion of Christ is seen
when we bring relief to help others who are suffering.

Keep honoring God and He will turn things around. I had to let go of how I thought my life would look and surrender. God is the master architect and builder, we can trust Him with our lives. Everything that broke my heart has driven me into a deeper relationship with the Lord. The heart break in my life drove me to seek the wisdom of God. He used my brokenness to develop my character and taught me to trust Him. God hears the cry of the broken. None of our struggles are wasted. Every lesson is powerful and will impact us forever. God opens doors, sends loving relationships, and support all around us. He brings us through to a flourishing finish.

CHAPTER 12

How Do I Forgive When I Don't Feel It?

But if you do not forgive men their trespasses,
neither will your Father forgive your trespasses.
Matthew 6:15 (NKJV)

How do I forgive someone when I'm still hurt? What do you do when you say: "I forgive them," but you still feel angry and hurt inside? The truth is forgiving others sets us free. Most of us have heard the saying: "Holding on to bitterness is like drinking poison and thinking it will harm the other person." It's important for us to forgive people, no matter how we feel about them. It's a decision of obedience to God. He said: "if we don't forgive, we won't be forgiven." If you want to be forgiven, you have to make the decision to forgive others. Do you want bitterness eating you up inside? Holding grudges gives a person power over you. Holding grudges hinders your destiny. Take your power back from the people who hurt you. Nothing and no one should have that much power over you, except God. Make a choice to forgive them. When the person comes to your mind, you can choose to forgive them by faith, in obedience to the Lord. Make Jesus Lord over all the negative thoughts and feelings. Make a decision to cast negative thoughts about other people down. Forget about it! If you'll do this God's way, eventually He will remove the negativity from your heart and mind. The people who hurt you are not more powerful than God. They can't stop God's plans for your life. Let God deal with it and move on. There is no limit to what God can do. God is able to remove everything that has tried to block, delay, or hinder His plans for your future.

Bitterness is a danger trap of the enemy to bring destruction in our life.

Several years ago I met an eighty year old woman in the mall. I began to share God's love with her. She told me that she had been abused by a nun when she was young. She was tormented by the memories. I asked her if the nun was still alive. She said: "no, she's been dead for years." I responded: "you're being controlled by a dead nun? She's dead and gone, but you're still allowing her to ruin your life; do you want to take your power back?" She said: "yes," we said a prayer together to release the hurt and bitterness. She made the choice at eighty years old to forgive and live in freedom. It's never too late as long as you're breathing.

Ask God for the grace to forgive others. Forgiving others means to release judgement against them and trust God to deal with the situation. Forgiving someone doesn't mean we have to remain connected to them. It doesn't mean we agree with what they've done. Forgiving others brings freedom. In no way does it mean that you need to stay with an abuser or return to a toxic, destructive, or dangerous situation. It means you make a choice to forgive and live in freedom. Satan will attempt to use the same situation over and over to keep stabbing you in the heart. Forgiving is an ongoing process. Letting go of offense toward others releases healing to our broken heart. Jesus taught on the power of forgiveness and healing.

God will remove the wrong people from your life. Instead of being hurt or angry, rejoice. You don't want anyone to hinder God's blessing in your future. Don't worry about a person who is trying to hold you back. Throw out the records of the wrongs. There is someone who has done everything right and that someone is JESUS. When you trust God, He will fight your battles for you and be with you in every trial to bring you through.

Nothing anyone has done to us can stop God from blessing us. God's plans for our lives are far greater than what anyone has done to hurt us. God is the one who will bring our dreams to pass. The God of the universe can turn things around in a split second. By forgiving others, they lose their power over us and we get to move on.

Forgiving is an ongoing process, not a one time event.

I once heard someone say: "a bad attitude is like a flat tire on a car, you can't go anywhere until you change it." Forgiving others allows us to move forward. No one is big enough to stop God's plans for your life.

For which is easier, to say, 'Your sins are forgiven you,'
or to say, 'Arise and walk'?
Matthew 9:5 (NKJV)

One of the hardest things to do is to forgive yourself. The devil brings guilt, condemnation, and shame. When the Holy Spirit convicts us, we repent and turn away from a negative behavior. Guilt, shame, and condemnation does not produce life. It's the devils counterfeit for godly sorrow. Repentance leads to salvation, restoration, and transformation. The devil is hard on everyone. He desires to poison your mind with negative self talk. He will use people to keep bringing up your past mistakes. The scripture tells us there is no condemnation for those who are in Christ Jesus. The law of life in Christ has set you free from the law of sin and death. When people bring up your past it's helpful to tell them that person doesn't exist anymore. "I'm a new creation in Christ Jesus. The old person is dead and gone."

Trying to hurt me by bringing up my past
is like trying to rob my old house. I don't live there anymore.

Jesus divinely connects receiving forgiveness for our sins to healing. One drop of the blood of Jesus is far more powerful than our mistakes or anyone else's. It's the old saying: "to err is human, but to forgive is divine." What the God of the universe has forgiven, has been washed away. Though yours sins were red like scarlet, they shall be as white as snow. God has removed your sin from you, as far as the east is from the west. Did you know the north and south meet up again, but the east and west never meet again? That's why the scriptures say He removed your sins from you as far as the east is from the west. God will never meet up with sin He has forgiven again. He threw your sins in a sea of forgetfulness. God said He will not remember your sins. Thank God for the power of the cross of Jesus Christ, which is the divine power to forgive and be forgiven. What Jesus accomplished on the cross is far greater than anyone's mistakes. Receive His grace to forgive yourself so you can heal and fulfill your divine purpose.

There have been times I've prayed for healing for people when the Lord revealed to me that they needed to forgive themselves. As soon as they forgave themselves their healing released.

The power of Jesus to forgive us,
destroys sins power to condemn us.

In the Hebrew language the name of Jesus is Yeshua. Yeshua means salvation. Salvation is His name. When you declare the name of Yeshua or the name of Jesus, you are declaring salvation.

Prayer For Salvation:
Heavenly Father I believe Jesus died on the cross to forgive me of my sins. He paid a sin debt I could never pay. I believe He rose from the grave, ascended into heaven, and is alive forevermore. I repent for my sins and ask Jesus to come into my heart, cleanse me and forgive me of my sins. I ask the Holy Spirit to fill me with power to become a new creation. Give me a willing and obedient heart. Empower me to follow Jesus all the days of my life, amen.

That if you confess with your mouth the Lord Jesus and believe in your heart that
God has raised Him from the dead, you will be saved.
For with the heart one believes unto righteousness, and with the mouth confession is
made unto salvation.
Romans 10:9-10 (NKJV)

Many people have faith to be saved through faith in the cross and blood of Jesus. If we have faith to be saved and forgiven, we should exercise the same faith to trust God to help us live in victory.

And be kind to one another, tenderhearted,
forgiving one another,
even as God in Christ forgave you.
Ephesians 4:32 (NKJV)

To humble ourselves and forgive others is good for us. It's part of our healing process. Let go of pride and all the records of wrong. Be honest enough to look in the mirror. Allow the Lord to begin healing your broken heart. It's time for a new beginning. The Bible teaches us that we are to lose sight of self, pick up our cross, and follow Jesus. Forget those things which are behind, press on to win the heavenly prize of God in Christ Jesus. Nothing and no one has the power to stop God from fulfilling His promise to us. No matter what has happened, it will turn around for our good. This makes it easier to forgive and trust God with all of our life. Remember Joseph was launched from the prison to the palace in on day. At the appointed time, God will perform His word. Thank you Lord.

CHAPTER 13

Vindication

Repay no one evil for evil. Have regard for good things in the sight of all men. If it is possible, as much as depends on you, live peaceably with all men. Beloved, do not avenge yourselves, but rather give place to wrath; for it is written, "Vengeance is Mine, I will repay," says the Lord.
Romans 12:17-19 (NKJV)

Vengeance is God's responsibility. Let Him deal with it.

Vindicate me, O God, And plead my cause against an ungodly nation;
Oh, deliver me from the deceitful and unjust man!
Psalm 43:1 (NKJV)

We are not to avenge ourselves
God will avenge us.

"But I say to you, love your enemies, bless those who curse you,
do good to those who hate you, and pray for those who
spitefully use you and persecute you."
Matthew 5:44 (NKJV)

Bless means to kneel and bless God as an act of adoration. We bless others as a benefit. Praying for blessings benefits everyone. One of the meanings of bless is to call down a blessing by prayer on those who persecute us.

Both Jesus and Stephen asked God to forgive their enemies moments before they died. They had an eternal perspective and didn't want God to charge them with their sin. We cannot imagine the majesty and splendor of heaven or the horrors and torment of hell. Having an eternal perspective transforms our heart toward our enemies.

Learning to bless those who curse us often begins by faith. Maybe you grew up around a lot of cursing, verbal abuse, and negativity. This would definitely be a foreign concept to you. It's a choice we make to forgive and bless. We may not feel the love that Jesus and Stephen felt instantly, but in time the Spirit of God will create a clean heart within us. We bless with our mouth and our heart begins to heal. It is faith working through love. Praying for our enemies is powerful.

Prayer for enemies:
Heavenly Father, I forgive them and ask You to do whatever is necessary to bring them out of darkness into the light. Give them a heart of true repentance so their sins will be forgiven and their lives will be transformed. Restrain them from any more wicked activities, so their attitude and choices will stop causing harm to themselves and others. Open their eyes to see the evil of their ways. Help them know the truth that will set them free. Soften their heart, removing hardness, rebellion, and stubbornness from it. Heal their broken heart. Reveal Jesus to them. Overshadow them with Your Holy Spirit. Touch their heart with Your perfect love. I ask You to send both human and angelic help in Jesus name, amen.

It would be a tremendous blessing to everyone to receive answers to these prayers!

The thief does not come except to steal, and to kill, and to destroy.
I have come that they may have life,
and that they may have it more abundantly.
John 10:10 (NKJV)

Satan brings evil and tries to get us to blame God. He attempts to get us to question God: "Did God really say it?" He twists and bends the truth. He is a liar and a deceiver.

When our hearts have been broken, Satan will attempt to use the trauma of an event that crushed us to wreak more havoc in our lives. This can cause reactions, bad memories, feelings of hopelessness, and worthlessness. It's a choice to guard our heart and trust God.

I've been through this one personally. I was so devastated by some of the circumstances God allowed. "God why would you let this happen to me?" I was completely worn out from the trials all around. Have you ever felt hemmed in, with no way out. Everywhere you turn there's another heart breaking situation. Sometimes God allows this to rearrange our course. He may be leading us in a new and different direction. Have you ever felt that you were at your wits end? Have you ever made a major decision and quickly regretted it? Most people have experienced some of this. The Israelites certainly did. They were hemmed in at the Red Sea, the Egyptian army chasing them, fear gripped their hearts. God certainly showed His power to deliver His people when they had no way of escape. God is faithful and He is no respecter of persons. That is really good news.

I was following a car years ago in California. The bumper sticker made a lasting impression on me, it said: "If You Don't Like The Direction Your Life Is Heading God Allows U-Turns." In the original language of the holy scriptures, there is no word for coincidence. God has many ways of speaking to us to get a point across.

In a time of great trial, God began to encourage me to write the books. People around me were encouraging me to write the books. I had many prophetic words regarding the books I would write and their impact. Dr. Francis Myles prophesied over me many years before I had written a book. He said: "The hand of God is heavy upon your life, the hand of God is heavy upon your life. Write the books, they will impact countless lives. God is going to breathe on them and give them wings to fly to the ends of the earth." Many people prophesied to me regarding the books I would write. There was so much confirmation. This book was written ten years after Dr. Myles spoke that word over me, then put on the shelf for another four years. I spent three of those four years pursuing a career in real estate. God prospered me tremendously and blessed me with favor.

Many of us experienced great changes when we were faced with Covid. It changed our world and impacted everyone. Sometimes God allows things to get hard to realign our priorities. We certainly see this throughout the pages of the Bible. God is always good. What seemed like a bad situation was God rearranging my life to fulfill what was in His heart. He gave me the time necessary to release the first of many books. God can use the most unusual circumstances to bring forth His blessing in our lives. This is one of the ways He heals our broken heart. God keeps His word to us. He is all powerful when we are powerless. God promised to restore us. He is forever faithful and trustworthy.

CHAPTER 14
Identifying Bitterness

Looking diligently lest any man fail of the grace of God;
lest any root of bitterness springing up trouble you,
and thereby many be defiled.
Hebrews 12:15 (KJV)

I had a serious situation with some people I had forgiven. I had been the bigger person for years. Many people would comment: "you were the bigger person again," every time I was around these individuals. I was going through a season of great trial. I let things get to me that I thought I had overcome. I was in extreme pain, to make matters worse the doctors put me on strong pain medications that made me much more reactive than normal during that period of time. I let the situation get into the ground of my heart. It began to impact my attitude. God began to show me that I was starting to operate in unforgiveness and that forgiving others must be an ongoing process. I started waking up thinking negative thoughts in the morning. I woke up in the morning thinking about what people had done to hurt me. I was rehearsing conversations. I would feel frustrated, disappointed, hurt, discouraged and negative. God showed me that I was being tormented by demons. He led me to a specific passage of scripture and had me study the deeper meaning behind the words. From that personal lesson I share this with you.

Looking diligently lest any man fail of the grace of God;
lest any root of bitterness springing up trouble you,
and thereby many be defiled.
Hebrews 12:15 (KJV)

Trouble in this passage means to be vexed, molested, and troubled by demons. Let no root of bitterness trouble you. Refuse to allow bitterness to control your life.

> *"Be angry, and do not sin":*
> *do not let the sun go down on your wrath,*
> *nor give place to the devil.*
> *Ephesians 4:26-27 (NKJV)*

We are supposed to make the decision to forgive others before we go to bed at night. When we don't do that a destructive process begins. The word devil means the slanderer. He is the accuser of the brethren, a deceiver, liar and thief. He will start to torment you. When we don't forgive before we go to bed, Satan will come and begin to torment us. He starts to plant evil thoughts in your mind, running negative tapes over and over again. It starts cooking you, it works into your subconscious mind which leads to being tormented by demons. They fill your mind with negative thoughts about other people. This releases negative emotion hormones from the brain into the superhuman highway of the body. This can cause your body to become a breeding ground for sickness and disease to grow.

> *Out of the same mouth proceed blessing and cursing.*
> *My brethren, these things ought not to be so.*
> *Does a spring send forth fresh water and bitter from the same opening?*
> *James 3:10-11 (NKJV)*

Bitterness causes a person to live in the pain of past hurts every single day. Waking up in the pain of the memory, feeling all the negative emotions over and over again. This keeps a person from a new day or living as a new creation. It's being held captive to negativity, being held as a prisoner of heartache. It's poison that will cause serious destruction to our lives. It is destructive to our mind, emotions, relationships, and every part of our life. It will also impact our decisions and hinder our destiny.

Let's take a look at some of the ways we can identify bitterness. I've had countless people come to me who were tormented by bitterness. From all of these experiences I created a check list to help people identify a root of bitterness.

- Do you wake up re-running the tapes of a bad situation over and over?
- Do you have a lot of regret about the past?

At some point we have to give up all regret about our past and trust God. God promises to take everything in our life and make something good out ALL of it. The blood of Jesus covers ALL of our life and is far more powerful than our mistakes or anyone else's.

One drop of the blood of Jesus is greater than
all the concentration of evil that has come against us.

- Is there someone you wake up thinking about constantly that hurt you?
- Do you repeat the same old stories over and over, recalling disappointments?
- Do you feel like you're always a victim?
- Do you blame others and avoid taking responsibility for your choices?
- Do you constantly bring up your dead past rehearsing negative events?
- Are you critical of others?

We read in our Bible that God forbids necromancy, which is speaking with the dead. Is your past dead? Make the decision to stop raising your dead past. Stop speaking to it. You can't go back and change the past, but you can change your future.

- Do you wish for bad things to happen to the people who you hurt you?
- Do you try to go after people to get vengeance?
- Do you withhold good that would help others?

"I'm not going to do anything for you, even though I know you need my help. I'm not going to help you unless I get my way." This is rooted in bitterness and selfishness.

- Do you try to destroy another person's reputation spreading gossip about them?

- Do you do things with the intention to hurt others?

"I'll show you." That is taking vengeance. Vengeance is cruelty that will affect every aspect of your own life. It is poison. The Bible clearly tells us NOT to do that. It is God's responsibility, not ours.

- Do you react or respond in a conflict?
- Is your natural reaction to get extremely defensive?
- When someone is difficult, how do you respond to them?
- Do you always go to the negative in a conflict instead of the positive?
- Is there a lot of strife and arguing with other people in your life?
- Are you critical and harsh toward other people?
- Do you explode in anger when you hear something you don't like?
- When you're confronted with an issue, do you turn and say something cruel to hurt the other person?

The answer to these questions help us to identify a root of bitterness. Bitterness allows the devil to snare us in a trap to poison our life. Bitterness causes a person to become tainted. Everything is viewed through a tainted, distorted, and twisted lens. There is a bending in their thinking. Bitterness causes a person to have a suspicious mind. To treat others with cruelty and harshness instead of love. Bitterness is a destroyer.

We can acknowledge that something a person has done to us is wrong without getting bitter. Our sins cost Jesus His life. To forgive and pray for our enemies sets us free.

When we focus on what hurt us we become self focused. When our thoughts are all about self, our light goes out and our life becomes dark. People who are self focused are miserable. When we turn our focus to God and being a blessing to others, our light shines. Finding ways to bless others fills our life with joy. We are the most like Jesus when we are generous to others, expecting nothing in return. When we focus on Jesus Christ we begin to see light shine in the darkness.

What about the people that just keep coming back to hurt you again and again? Jesus taught us to forgive them seventy times seven. That number is boundless, keep forgiving them. Forgiving others is good for us. This is a decision all of us must make. Forgiving others is actually doing something good for yourself. Forgiving is truly a blessing that leads to a brighter tomorrow. Remember nothing anyone has done to hurt you is more powerful than God's ability to bless you. Shift your focus to God's supernatural power and trust Him with it. Let it go and move on.

**Don't allow your past to keep you from your future.
You can't move forward looking back.**

There are people who tell you the same negative stories over and over. There was a homeless man I hadn't seen for years. When I saw him again, he told me the same tragic story I heard years prior. There are many lives poisoned by the pain in their past. I saw this repeatedly when I was trying to help the homeless. Most were tormented by trauma from their past.

When bitterness develops a root system in our heart, it will adversely affect every aspect of our lives. It's crucial to uproot bitterness from our lives so God can heal our broken heart.

One of the ways to heal a broken heart is to let go of what is destructive to us. Everyone won't like or love us. Some people aren't going to like us no matter what we do. Don't waste anymore time or energy on negative things that have happened in the past. It's time to take your power back and press on.

We can't get to a bright future, stuck in our dead past. The past is gone, there's nothing anyone can do to change it, but we can change how we approach each new day. Forget what's behind you! Let God deal with your past. If we're going to fulfill our purpose we've got to understand that where we're heading in the future is more important than what happened in the past.

Brethren, I do not count myself to have apprehended;
but one thing I do, forgetting those things which are behind and reaching forward to
those things which are ahead, I press toward the goal for the prize of the upward
call of God in Christ Jesus.
Philippians 3:13-14 (NKJV)

I hope you get a personal revelation of the unlimited power of God to bless and restore your life. Make the decision to forget the past. No one is greater than God. Christ has the power to take everything that was working against you and turn it around for good. He is all powerful, God wants to heal and restore your life.

Prayer:
Father forgive me for allowing bitterness to grow in my heart. I'm sorry, I repent. I release all the negativity. I choose to forgive myself and others. I give up all regret about my life. Teach me the lesson you have for me, I don't have to go through this again. Show me the good things You have planned. Create in me a clean heart and renew a right Spirit within me. I refuse to allow this situation to rule my life one more day. I ask You to uproot every trace of bitterness in my heart. Help me to stop recalling disappointment. Help me to win the battle in my mind. Empower me to stop rehearsing negative things that happened in the past. Thank You for Your transforming power to set me free. I ask for the grace to forgive myself and others. Thank You for redeeming me from the curse. Thank You for translating me out of the kingdom of darkness into the Kingdom of Your Son, in whom I have redemption and forgiveness of sins. Thank You for delivering me out of difficulty into peace. I receive the power of the cross, Your grace to be forgiven and extend forgiveness to others. Thank You Jesus for setting me free. Thank You for delivering me from evil. Thank You for ordering my steps and arranging divine appointments. Thank You for Your perfect plans for my life. Thank You for working all things for my good. Thank You for breathing new life into me. Thank You for sending Jesus to heal my broken heart, bind up my wounds and make me whole. Thank You for restoration in Jesus name, amen.

The scriptures reveal that David made many mistakes in his life. David was a man after God's own heart. David did not get bitter over his mistakes or the way other people treated him. When David made a mistake, he ran to the mercy of God. He ran to God to seek forgiveness and grace to help him in his time of need. He understood that it's better to trust God than man. David believed that no matter how bad things got, he would live to see the goodness of the Lord in his life. He understood that God could heal his broken heart and make something beautiful out of his broken life and God did just that.

He who sins is of the devil, for the devil has sinned from the beginning.
For this purpose the Son of God was manifested,
that He might destroy the works of the devil.
1 John 3:8 (NKJV)

Jesus came to destroy the works of the devil.

No one had more reasons to carry offense than Jesus. He was rejected, despised, falsely accused, beaten, betrayed, endured the most corrupt criminal trial in history and was crucified.

When Jesus rose from the grave,
He never recalled the traumatic events that led to His crucifixion

Real power is self control. Jesus did not recall disappointment. He is the most masculine and powerful man that has ever lived. Jesus exemplifies the power of self control in His life, death, and resurrection. Jesus is our role model. Jesus walked out of the grave with absolute power and authority. When we lose sight of self, willingly dying to self, we come alive in Jesus. He will give us the power to let go of the pain of the past so we can live each new day with victory.

CHAPTER 15
Refuse The Blame Game

For I acknowledge my transgressions…
Psalm 51:3 (NKJV)

In Psalm 51 David receives a correction from the prophet Nathan. He had taken another man's wife, Bathsheba. He intentionally sent her husband to the front lines of battle where he was killed. David attempted to cover it up. When God sent Nathan to confront David, he did not play the blame game. David owned his mistake and repented. He ran to the mercy of God, not from Him.

Repentance leads to restoration. True repentance means you don't go back. You don't do it again. You leave it and move on. When we humble ourselves and repent, God is faithful to cleanse and restore our lives.

Many people blame others for everything. Many are masters at flipping the script in every conflict. Narcissistic abusers are master manipulators, they fight dirty. Dirty fighters always attack others personally with hurtful remarks in a disagreement. This is a manipulation tactic that keeps them from looking in the mirror and dealing with real issues. There is only one way to deal with a dirty fighter, stay out of the ring. If you go in the ring with a dirty fighter, you will have to become a master at reframing conversations. When a conflict arises with a dirty fighter they attack you personally. They will tell you everything they think is wrong with you. There will be verbal bashing and character assassination that leaves you emotionally devastated. They are master manipulators. They will run you over like a bulldozer. They will accuse you of what they are doing, which is also known as gaslighting. They operate in self deception and control. They wipe people out emotionally. They are emotional terrorists. A person must overcome the hurt and stay focused on what the real issues are in order to bring the conversation back around to resolve the conflict.

The dirty fighter is a character assassin. A person has to put aside their feelings to deal with a dirty fighter and stay focused. The dirty fighter is an abuser. Some people will avoid dealing with any issues with a dirty fighter because it's so hurtful and exhausting. They would rather walk away from the person longing for peace.

The dirty fighter will abuse their power over others. They use control, manipulation, intimidation, domination, threats, and deception in an attempt to get their way. They are masters at flipping the script to put blame on others. They abuse others and pretend they are the victim. They demand their way and if they don't get it, there will be hell to pay. They are filled with pride and self deception. They will keep a record of what they have done for you. This will be used as a weapon of choice against you when a conflict arises. They violate healthy boundaries and invade your privacy in their quest to get their way and control your life. They will misuse their power and money to manipulate, control, and abuse others. They will put you under their thumb if given the opportunity. They have completely misplaced loyalty.

Blaming others does not help anyone get well. I have lived through many difficult circumstances. Some circumstances were the result of my choices, others were the actions of others in which I had no control. God keeps accurate records so we don't have to. It's really about letting go and trusting God to deal with all of our life. I honestly felt like Job for many years. I even said: "Lord if you slay me I will still love you." That was right before a season of great change in my life.

God does not hold us responsible for what others do, but we are accountable for how we respond. Sometimes we blow it and have to repent. Godly sorrow promotes prosperity in our soul. We are given many opportunities to develop our character. When we do what we can, God will do what we can't. Forgiving others instead of blaming them is real freedom.

The dirtiest of fighters are often bold faced liars and manipulators, but they cannot stop God's blessing. No one has enough power to stop the God who runs the universe from doing what He has promised. The knowledge of this truth gives us the power to let go and move on. God knows the truth and eventually the truth will rise to the top.

CHAPTER 16
Avoid - Deny - Abuse

And you shall know the truth, and the truth shall make you free."
Experiencing the truth personally will free you.
John 8:32 (NKJV)

There is a pattern called Avoid - Deny - Abuse
Until we acknowledge our pain, we won't be able to heal.

Avoid, deny, abuse patterns cause people to continuously sweep matters of the heart under the rug. The problem is eventually it will come out in an unhealthy way, if we refuse to deal with it in a healthy manner.

Many people are in denial by choice. This is how they avoid facing the truth about themselves. It's how they avoid what shattered their dreams and broke their heart. Sometimes we avoid an issue in an attempt to protect ourselves and others. We don't want to hurt and we don't want to hurt anyone else. A conflict may be uncomfortable for a moment, but everyone benefits when we resolve issues and get healed.

Some people have been deceived into believing that by avoiding and denying the pain in their heart, they are protecting themselves from being hurt more. There is often great disappointment, fear, and shame associated with what has broken our heart. People try to minimize their pain in many different ways. Avoiding and denying are a few of those ways.

Often a person who makes the choice to avoid and deny will run from one relationship to another. They might keep an unusually busy schedule or sink deep into a place of loneliness and depression wanting to be left alone. This causes even more suffering.

A person can't heal pretending they're doing well. Trying to disconnect yourself from the truth delays your freedom. Truth sets us free. Many people attempt to disconnect from the truth about themselves. We can't bury our head in the sand, we have to face the truth so God can heal us.

Avoid, deny, abuse is a real pattern that leads to more heart break. The abuse could be verbal abuse, drug abuse, alcohol abuse and on and on. Avoid, deny, abuse is a pattern of a person who is hiding in darkness. This contaminates our life.

If you sweep the dirt in your house under the rug everyday, eventually there will be a mountain of dirt. It will become visible. It's like Mount St. Helens, avoiding and denying will eventually lead to a very serious eruption.

The best decision we can make is to be courageous and honest about ourselves and our pain. God will heal our broken heart when we let Him. When we allow God into the place of our brokenness, we will begin to heal and experience healthy love.

To avoid and deny never brings peace, never solves a conflict, and can never heal our broken heart. What this pattern does is keep a person's heart locked up in a prison of darkness. This keeps a person bound up as a type of spiritual prisoner. Jesus came to set the captives free from confinement, condemnation, physical and spiritual captivity, and bring freedom to prisoners. He came to heal the brokenhearted and bind up our wounds. Jesus exemplifies extravagant love in action.

Have you ever struggled when things weren't going your way and thought; "what's wrong with me? Why can't I breakthrough? Am I damaged beyond what you can bless God?" The answer is no! No one is too far gone for God's love and grace. The devil is a liar. He is the accuser of the brethren. He doesn't want you to know how precious and valuable you are to God and others. It's my hope that you'll become aware of the depth of God's love for you. He can heal all the trauma, disappointment, and hurt. Give Jesus all the baggage. You don't need to carry it anymore.

In some support groups there's an overemphasis on rehearsing the past, constantly sharing the same negative stories. This is harmful because it keeps a person reliving negativity instead of trusting God with it and moving on. A person can get stuck if they are continually rehearsing negative events.

....[and cease recalling disappointments].
Psalm 48:13 (AMPC)

God's mercy is new every morning. Look for something good to focus on everyday instead of brooding over negativity from behind you, it's a healthy choice.

There comes a time when no matter what's happened to us, we have to face the mirror. We have to take responsibility for our own lives and allow God to transform us. We can make a decision to refuse to blame others. Refuse to be offended. This might be where I am today, but I am not going to stay here. I'm getting rid of all the negativity and limitations and allowing God to create a future full of hope. I receive the amazing love of God. We can trust God to give us restitution. God is able to recompense us for all the loss and suffering in our life.

Trust God to lead you to an expected end.

Many people are paralyzed by some kind of fear. What would you do if you had no fear? The answer to that question reveals what fear is restricting you from having and enjoying in life.

David talked to God about every painful struggle in his life. He expressed himself to God even more when he felt weak, defeated, heart broken, or troubled. The book of Psalms is a great way to learn to express your heart to God. I encourage you to read the Psalms out loud.

A Psalm of David.
How long, O Lord? Will You forget me forever?
How long will You hide Your face from me?
How long shall I take counsel in my soul,
Having sorrow in my heart daily?
How long will my enemy be exalted over me? Consider and hear me,
O Lord my God; Enlighten my eyes, Lest I sleep the sleep of death;
Lest my enemy say, "I have prevailed against him"; Lest those who trouble me
rejoice when I am moved. But I have trusted in Your mercy;
My heart shall rejoice in Your salvation. I will sing to the Lord,
Because He has dealt bountifully with me.
Psalm 13 (NKJV)

The Joy of the Lord is our source of strength. There comes a time when no matter what we've been through, we have to take responsibility for our lives and let healing flow. The blame game is a dead end street. No one will live a perfect life. Everyone gets hurt, trouble comes to everyone. When we are honest and allow God to work in our heart, He can and will deal bountifully with us. God intends to take our past, present, and future and use it for our good and for His glory. He desires to give us a story of triumph. God has perfect timing and a perfect plan for our lives. We trust the Lord to save us, we can trust Him to break every negative cycle from our past. We experience the sustaining power of God as He brings us through difficulty. We can trust God will all of our life.

The people who had the greatest favor in the Bible
endured the most extreme trials.

Their lives are an example of God's limitless and surpassing power to turn things around. God allowed their difficult circumstances to reveal His great and mighty power over everything. When we are down to nothing, God is always up to something good. God can make something out of nothing. He can do amazing things. He allows maximum brokenness so we can make maximum impact. Joseph, David, Paul, and Jesus are all beautiful examples of this truth. God turned the negative into a positive for them and He will do it for you too.

We were born to be a light in the world.

We can't have a new beginning holding on to our dead past. It is crucial that we let go of what is behind us so we can start a new day. Ask God to help you give up all regret about your life and trust Him with your future.

"Do not remember the former things, Nor consider the things of old.
Behold, I will do a new thing ...
Isaiah 43:18-19 (NKJV)

God said: "I will doing a new thing!" He did not say: "Hey, I was thinking about doing something new." God said: "Behold, I will do a new thing." You can declare it: "Lord I receive the new thing You are doing in my life today."

Not one of us can get the years back that broke our heart. We can't go back and make the wrongs right. What can we do? Make the decision to STOP thinking about the past. STOP talking about it unless it's how things have turned around for our good. God receives glory from turning our tragedy to triumph.

Prayer:
Heavenly Father help me to stop thinking about negative events in the past. Thank You for the good plans You have for me. You are my living hope. Let faith arise within my heart and mind. Thank You for giving me strength to overcome in every situation in Jesus name, amen.

CHAPTER 17
Grace To Help
In My Time Of Need

Let us therefore come boldly to the throne of grace,
that we may obtain mercy
and find grace to help in time of need.
Hebrews 4:16 (NKJV)

Notice it's not the absence of a need, it's in the time of our need we go boldly to God's throne of Grace to obtain mercy and grace to help. Mercy is compassion. Jesus moves with compassion to help us in our time of need. His compassion and grace bring help and relief in our time of affliction and suffering.

God's throne of Grace is the highest position of authority.

Jesus gave us access to God's throne of grace. God is far above every circumstance, struggle, and situation you're facing right now. He has the power to turn it around in your favor. The Bible says we are seated in heavenly places with Christ Jesus. That is the seat of mercy and grace. We can sit down and find rest with Christ and God will fight for us. God's grace was given in Christ Jesus. Grace is God giving His good and perfect gifts to humanity. When we lean on God's grace, it takes pressure off of us.

Grace is the forgiveness, generosity, lovingkindness, compassion and favor of God. Experiencing God's grace is so powerful, it empowers us to stop leaning toward negativity. Grace causes us to receive the goodness of God.

Grace is God's compassion and kindness bestowed upon us that we don't deserve. Jesus won God's favor for us at the cross. By grace we are saved. God is gracious even when we don't deserve it. You could have messed things up so badly, you feel like the most underserving and wicked sinner. You can come to God and the power of grace is given for you to repent, own up to your mistakes, and admit that you've been wrong. Ask God to forgive you and stop the pain and suffering in your life. He is looking and longing to be gracious to you. Ask God to turn things around in your favor. Call upon Jesus and ask Him to fill you with His Holy Spirit to enable you to live a life of obedience. Ask God to help you fulfill your divine purpose. Accomplishing what God created you to do is the most rewarding experience in this life. No one knows you better than Almighty God. His purpose for your life is the reason you're alive.

**Grace is God revealing His will for your life
and empowering you to achieve it.**

God's grace moves to tilt the scales in our favor. God's grace and mercy is available to us right now. God gives us rewards and blessings we don't deserve and withholds the punishment we do deserve. Through faith in Christ, grace takes us just as we are and begins to transform our lives. Grace is God giving us beauty for ashes. God takes the biggest mess and brings forth a message that brings hope and healing to countless lives. Grace is the kindness of God conferring divine favor on the least deserving among us. Grace is God granting pardon to us for our sin and offenses and offering us eternal salvation through faith in Christ.

God is the master in kindness. His mercy is given that we can be forgiven and extend that same forgiveness to others. May God's grace flow to us and through us. May we obtain all the kindness, generosity, and goodness of God that Jesus made available to us.

God's grace can put you in a position you didn't earn, that you were not even qualified for. God's grace causes the person who is the least likely to succeed to obtain honor an influence, like Joseph. No one would expect a future leader to emerge from the prison, but God. Grace is when God brings you from the back to the front because He knows what He placed inside of you. Grace is obtaining God's peace in the midst of personal loss and difficulty.

God's grace supersedes your stature, financial status, family history, education, location, or limitations. Your blessing is because of God's supernatural power and ability. Grace is God granting you favor and causing your dreams to be fulfilled.

Grace is the power of God that removes difficulty, replacing it with stability. Grace is God moving in our circumstances, blessing us beyond anything we could have imagined. Grace is God's supernatural strength made perfect in our weakness. Grace is experiencing the surpassing greatness and goodness of Almighty God. God's grace is given so we can live a productive life and accomplish His will. We aren't saved to sit around. We are saved and given grace to be productive and fulfill our purpose.

My grace is sufficient for you, for my strength is made perfect in weakness.
2 Corinthians 12:9 (NKJV)

Where we are weak, His grace is the strength of our life.

What we can't accomplish without the power of God's grace, we are supernaturally empowered to accomplish through His grace. Turn to God and ask him to be the master in kindness, mercy, grace, and power in your life.

Prayer:
Heavenly Father, I bless and praise You. Thank You for Your amazing grace. There is no one like You. It's all about what Jesus has done. Thank You for bringing relief in my time of affliction and suffering. Empower me to fulfill all Your good plans for my life. Thank You for Your supernatural power, protection, and provision in my life and my family. Thank You for encouraging me daily so I can encourage others. Show me who I can bless today. Make me an answer. Thank You for giving me solutions to problems. Thank You Lord that Your grace and mercy are part of my covenant relationship, sealed in the blood of Jesus. I'm grateful that You are a rewarder. I receive all that You have for me. Thank You for Your perfect love. Thank You Lord for empowering me

to trust You. Thank You for hearing my prayers. Thank You that my life and times are in Your hands. I ask You to release your favor, blessing, and grace that causes me to show Your love and compassion to humanity. Thank You for well timed help coming just when I need it. May Your favor, grace, and mercy influence my character and conduct. I humbly rely on Your grace and mercy. I ask You to help me overcome distractions, disappointment, heartache, and sorrow. I ask for discernment and wisdom Lord. Bless me to be a blessing. Give me a willing and obedient heart. Thank You for Your generous heart. I am grateful for all You've done for me. Thank You for blessing me beyond measure. Thank You for allowing me to see Your goodness everywhere I go in Jesus name, amen.

CHAPTER 18
Thank God For What You Do Have

Thank You Is The Password

Enter into His gates with thanksgiving,
And into His courts with praise.
Be thankful to Him, and bless His name.
Psalm 100:4 (NKJV)

God spoke to my heart as I was writing this book about the importance of being thankful for what we have. Why would God want to give us more to murmur and complain about? One of the keys to overcoming negativity is to be thankful. A heart of gratitude is a beautiful attribute of God's grace.

As parents we aren't likely to reward our children with more, if they're complaining about what we gave them. It's a joy to reward our children when they show gratitude. Do you think God is going to give us more to complain about? He is not going to do that. God gives us more, when we give thanks for what we have.

What would you do if the only thing you would have tomorrow, is what you thanked God for today? I know what I would do. I would count every blessing and thank God for everything and everyone in my life. If you knew that being thankful would open doors to your destiny, would you start thanking God right now? An attitude adjustment can change the course of our lives.

If you complain you remain. Thank you is the password that opens doors to brighter days. An attitude of gratitude gives us wings to soar to new heights. Complaining brings death to our progress. It's the opposite of being thankful. People died in the Old Testament for complaining. God took it personally. I'm not saying you will die for it, but it will stop your progress dead in its tracks.

Nor complain, as some of them also complained,
and were destroyed by the destroyer.
1 Corinthians 10:10 (NKJV)

Praise God for everything you can think of when you feel like complaining. This creates a new habit, a new way of living. Start with one thing you can think of that you're thankful for. You'll find yourself going down a long list before you're done with all the reasons you have to be grateful.

When I was struggling I caught myself complaining. I was starting to have an attitude of defeat. It's dangerous to complain, yet easy to do when we are broken and discouraged by difficult circumstances in our life. I began to feel negative. I had to make a conscious decision to refuse to complain and replace it with praise. I would stop myself before I would say something and speak the opposite of what I was feeling. I would speak words of gratitude and victory, but I was not feeling that way at the time. The battle is real. We win with God's word.

Being thankful is an instant mood elevator.

Prayer:
Heavenly Father, I thank You for Your faithfulness. You are an awesome God. I love You. I give You the highest praise. Thank You for keeping Your promises. Thank You for Your mercy and compassion. Thank You for loving me and never letting me go. Thank You for my family and all the wonderful people in my life. Thank You for my health and all the gifts You've given me. Thank You for success in my life. Thank You for Your power, presence, and majesty. Thank You for pouring forth blessings and perfecting the things that concern me. Thank You for energizing and equipping me to work hard and succeed. Thank You that my path is getting brighter and brighter. Thank You

for wisdom and discernment. Thank You for divine protection over my life and family. Thank You for performing Your word. Thank You for transforming my life and making all things beautiful. Thank You for giving me beauty for ashes. Thank You Lord for giving me a bright future, hope, and an expected end. Let this mind be in me, that was in Christ Jesus. Thank You for giving me wisdom to make good decisions. Thank You Lord for giving back all the enemy has stolen with interest. Thank You for a good inheritance. Thank you for refining me through the pressures in life. Thank You for giving me a heart to love the broken. Thank You for everything that has brought me to this new day. Your joy gives me strength. Thank You for abundant provision for all my needs and beyond, so I can dispense good to others. The Lord is my Shepherd, I shall not want. I hear Your voice and follow You. Thank You Jesus for Your life of obedience. Thank You for Your stripes, blood, cross, and resurrection power that I could have and enjoy life, and have it in abundance to the full, till it overflows. Thank You for filling me with joy and gratitude today. Thank You for giving me a new heart. I am a new creation in Christ. I am the redeemed of the Lord and I say so. I believe the report of the Lord. Thank You for restoring my life and healing me. Thank You Lord that nothing and no one can stop Your blessing in my life. Thank You for rendering my enemies harmless against me. Your plans for my life are coming to pass. Thank You for great favor everywhere I go. Thank You for everything and everyone you have blessed me with in my life. Thank You for divine connections. Thank You for blessing me to be a blessing in Jesus name, amen.

You have power over your mind. With God's help, you can change your mind. Ask God to help you overcome negative thought patterns. When a negative thought comes, cast it down and meditate on God's word. Instead of speaking the negative emotion you're feeling, say the opposite. Speak life, your words are powerful. We have to train our mind and mouth to be thankful everyday.

In everything give thanks;
for this is the will of God in Christ Jesus for you.
1 Thessalonians 5:18 (NKJV)

Gratitude is a beautiful attribute of the grace of God.

CHAPTER 19

I Surrender - I Have Decided To Trust You God

God allowed many incredible experiences in my life as well as many devastating circumstances. He used all of it to mold and shape me. Through the most difficult circumstances, God gave me a heart of great compassion for those suffering. I learned that we have to make a conscience decision to forget the past and what other people have done to hurt us. We have to forgive ourselves and others and let go of all the mistakes. God see's the greatness He placed inside of us when others don't. God is arranging your destiny. Nothing could stop God's blessing in Joseph's life. Nothing stopped God's blessing in David's life. Nothing and no one is powerful enough to stop Almighty God from restoring our lives, when we trust and obey Him. No one can curse what God has blessed. Obedience releases us into God's blessing.

Trust God with everything you've been through. Get excited about the future and all the wonderful people you are about to connect with. Refuse to allow fear and bitterness in your life. Trauma, fear, and bitterness open the door to demonic activity and demonic strongholds. We can be sincere, but be sincerely wrong. Jesus came to deliver us from evil. He is the mender of the broken.

Prayer:
Heavenly Father, You are all powerful. You are The Great I Am. You are absolute authority. There is no one like You. I place my heart in your hands. I don't understand many things that have happened to me, but I've made up my mind to trust You. I surrender all of my life to You. You are a great and mighty

God. I know You are with me and You are for me. Thank You for keeping track of all my sorrow and collecting my tears in Your bottle. I give You all of my mistakes and everyone else's. I give you all the pain and trauma in my life. I ask You to deliver me from evil and every demonic stronghold. I place my broken heart in Your hands. I give You everything. Thank You for healing my broken heart. Thank You for giving me beauty for ashes. Thank You for restoring my life and making all things beautiful. Thank You for revealing Your great and mighty love and awesome power to me. Thank You for the privilege to know You. Thank You for this life Lord. Thank You for empowering me to fulfill my destiny. Thank You for every person I have the privilege to share Your love with. Thank You for every lesson in my life. Thank You for anointing me with power. Great is Your faithfulness to me. Thank You Lord. I love and trust You in Jesus name, amen.

God is no respecter of persons. What he did for David he will do for you. Run to God for help instead of running from Him. Talk to God about every struggle. God knows the struggle is real. He never called any of us to walk this journey alone. We need each other. Let down the walls of self protection that keep wonderful people and blessings out of your life.

I could not have written this book without many wonderful people who have loved, supported, encouraged, and helped me along the way. I know the pain of broken dreams, physical health struggles, and devastating circumstances beyond our control. The good news is that God does not leave us there. God gives us grace and help in our time of need. God provides our needs. God fills our life with wonderful, loving people and surprises. He gives us strength to work hard and overcome.

I'm the least among you, but God is great. Whatever God has called us to do, He wants to bless and prosper. God is able to give us strength in our weakness. He has not forgotten us. He is with us in the fire, He is with us in the flood. He is forever faithful and true. God longs to heal our broken heart and bind up our wounds, every moment of every day. He will take what the devil meant for evil against us and turn it around for our good. He will make all things beautiful in His time, because of His great and mighty love. No one can take God's promise from you. Look for ways to be a blessing to other people. Keep doing what God has called you to do with a good attitude. Do whatever you're doing with all your heart. God will reward you. He is a generous and faithful God.

Jesus came to heal our broken heart and make us whole again. So many people need healing for their broken heart. So many people need hope. No one has sunk so deep that God's love is not deeper. No one is beyond God's reach. Run into the everlasting arms of God. Let the lavish love of God heal every fragment in your heart. He longs to put you back together and give you a powerful story of victory that will help many other people.

I hope you will make a decision to trust God, even when you don't understand the painful things that have happened in your life. We don't have to understand, we have to trust God. No one knows how God is running the universe, but He is. The sun, moon and stars aren't crashing into each other. God is all powerful and the giver of every good and perfect gift. The God who upholds the universe wants to heal your broken heart. This passage is very helpful in letting go and learning to trust God.

Trust in the Lord with all your heart,
And lean not on your own understanding;
In all your ways acknowledge Him, And He shall direct your paths.
Proverbs 3:5-6 (NKJV)

The scriptures tell us how Joseph's dream turned into a nightmare. It appeared that everything was working against him. Joseph endured one terrible event after another. Many people would have thought God had left Joseph during those years. He endured so much hardship and tragedy. However, all of it was part of God's plan. Joseph was catapulted out of the prison into the palace in one day. Joseph became a great ruler over a nation. He became the Prime Minister of Egypt, second in command. Joseph's dreams were realized. The journey to the fulfillment of his dreams was not what he would have imagined, but God fulfilled His word to Joseph. The place Joseph endured great injustice was God's springboard into his destiny. Joseph was called out of the prison to stand before the Pharaoh, the ruler of the nation in one day. We serve the God of the suddenly. He is a miracle working God.

If your dreams have turned upside down, remember Joseph. God may be putting someone in your life that is connected to your destiny. God is arranging your future. Joseph met Pharaoh's cupbearer in prison. Joseph begged him to remember him, but he forgot Joseph for two long years. That must have been extremely disappointing. God made sure the cupbearer remembered Joseph by giving Pharaoh dreams that no one could interpret. In the end it was all a set up. God divinely connected Joseph in the most unusual way. Everything that appeared to be sent to stop God's plans for his future, was actually a divine set up. We have to keep a good attitude and continue to use the gifts God has given us to bless and help others. As we continue to work hard and find ways to help solve problems for others, God will do the same for us. God's grace gives us the power to live a productive life of obedience.

Most of us have heard the saying: "The problem you solve for others determines your value," it's true. Jesus solved our biggest problem, paying a sin debt none of us could pay. He is seated in heaven in the highest position of authority and honor. Joseph solved a problem for two men in prison that led to solving the Pharaoh's problem. The launching pad to Joseph's dreams was not what he would have imagined.

Through adversity Joseph learned to depend on God regardless of the circumstances!

There are over seven billion people in the world today. Don't allow one person or group of people who don't believe in you to keep you from your destiny. No matter how long it's been, or what you're going through right now, don't give up. Continue to work toward the dream God has placed in your heart and keep a good attitude. God will eventually show up for you. Difficulty is not an indication that God has left you or that He doesn't love you. It may be a divine set up by God to launch you into your purpose. In Genesis Chapter 41 the cupbearer remembered Joseph who was still in prison. This was hardly a place anyone expected a future leader to emerge from. Joseph was remembered that day, in the day of his hardship. It was the appointed time. Joseph didn't have a cell phone, a computer, an instagram account, an impressive wardrobe, a home, or a vehicle. Joseph had been stripped down to nothing, yet God launched

Joseph from the most difficult place in his life into a position of great influence and blessings. Joseph's dreams came true in one day, although the preparation for that day had taken years.

Don't allow anything or anyone to rob you of your dreams. God has a future and hope for each and every one of us. God can render everything that has come against your destiny powerless. Continue to use the gifts God has given you to encourage others and trust God. Continue to do the right thing, even when the wrong thing happens. God will vindicate you. Look for ways to be a blessing. Be an answer to someone else's problem. There is so much joy in giving. God is a rewarder. He is a God of justice.

God will cause people to remember us in His perfect time. God will launch us into our destiny to fulfill our dreams. Joseph suffered adversity until God sufficiently tried his patience and developed his character. Great adversity is a sign that the assignment God has for your life is more significant than you may have imagined. What others meant against us to bring harm, God will use to bring good, to preserve and save lives.

But as for you, you meant evil against me; but God meant it for good,
in order to bring it about as it is this day, to save many people alive.
Genesis 50:20 (NKJV)

And we know that all things work together
for good to those who love God,
to those who are the called according to His purpose.
Romans 8:28 (NKJV)

God is working our yesterday, today,
and tomorrow out for good.

Be of good courage,
And He shall strengthen your heart,
All you who hope in the Lord.
Psalm 31:24 (NKJV)

Heal me, O Lord, and I shall be healed;
Save me, and I shall be saved, For You are my praise.
Jeremiah 17:14(NKJV)

The trials in life are intended to teach us to trust the Lord.
We learn to depend on the surpassing greatness of His power

Joseph told his brothers, you meant it for evil against me; but God meant it for good to save many people's lives. I pray that everyone who reads this book would come to that place of absolute forgiveness and freedom. Whatever others meant to cause evil, God meant it for good.

No one can stop God from blessing us when we keep our heart free from offense and continue to do God's will. I hope you will be of good courage and allow God to strengthen your heart as you put your hope in the Lord. Jesus came to seek and to save the lost. To destroy the works of the devil and to heal the brokenhearted. God is a God of restoration. Jesus is the Lord of the breakthrough. God is able to turn the tables in your favor. Believe that restoration will come to you. God is able to fulfill His original intention for your life.

When God restores you, He gives back what was stolen with interest. God is a God of justice. God will restore honor where honor has been withheld. He will establish you in His grace, provision, purpose, promise and goodness. Ask God to tilt the scales in your favor. God will cause someone to remember you. Remember things turned around suddenly for Joseph. In one day he went from the prison to the palace. I hope this encourages you. You could have a breakthrough that changes your life in 24 hours like Joseph. God performs miracles every moment of every day. He never sleeps or slumbers.

No one can stop God from blessing us at the appointed time. There is a date set for the release of God's promise, purpose, restoration, vindication and rewards. In one day Joseph was rewarded with the spoils of Egypt. God rewarded Joseph for the adversity and heart break he endured. God rewarded Joseph for being a man of integrity, kindness, and compassion. Joseph showed kindness to others in prison. He moved with compassion when two men were troubled by their dreams. Joseph used the gifts God had given him to encourage those men and interpret their dreams. He was careful to give glory to God. He told them that interpretation comes from God. Because of that one act of kindness, Pharaoh's cupbearer would eventually remember Joseph. This would be the divine connection that launched Joseph into his destiny. God restored Joseph and vindicated him. He knows how to heal broken hearts and bind up our wounds. God brings relief, healing, and restores our fortunes.

Nothing anyone did to hurt Joseph could stop God from blessing him, because Joseph refused to get negative or bitter. It is so important we show kindness, compassion, and love to others. Continue to honor God and look for ways to bless other people. God will cause someone in a key position to remember you, at the right time. God will provide opportunities and promotion. You won't have to go looking for opportunities, God will bring opportunities to you. No one can stop your destiny if you will forgive others and keep working hard. Never forget that no one is big enough to stop your destiny when you trust God and obey Him.

Don't worry about the people who are showing contempt toward you, who disrespect you. God caused the people that showed contempt and disrespect toward Joseph to honor and respect him. God is watching everything that people are doing. God is watching everything. Nothing escapes His watchful eye. Some people may think they're getting away with being deceptive and nasty, but in the end God will have the last say in the matter. It's all in God's perfect timing. God can change the way people see you. He is no respecter of persons. What He has done for others, He will do for you. Continue to forgive others, show kindness, be generous and keep a good attitude.

Someone else's negative attitude cannot strip God's promise from our life. When we allow the heart break we've endured to serve as our teacher, we become rich in wisdom. Hardship is not an indication that God's favor has left you, it's an indication that God has great things in your future. Remember God keeps accurate records and He will reward you for continuing to honor Him. God will vindicate you against those who caused you harm. God will promote you, He will cause those who dishonored you to see you in a new light. God will make sure that eventually you will receive the respect that you deserve.

God's blessing will come forth because no one is powerful enough to stop His blessing. Trust God and He will bless you greatly to fulfill your destiny. God will turn your mourning into dancing. He promised to give us beauty for ashes. He promised that weeping may endure for a night, but joy comes in the morning. Joseph's hopes were deferred for a time but the answer came. That answer is a tree of life. God gives us divine favor to carry on in the midst of adversity.

During the years I was suffering in hardship, many people told me that when they blessed me, God began to bless them with increase. Their business increased, their children got promotions, and their health improved. Many shared testimonies of miracles and healing during those years. That was the blessing of the Lord. God is amazing.

No matter what kind of shaking we go through, God remains the anchor to our soul and the rock on which we stand. Our suffering doesn't last forever. God puts us back on our feet and blesses the work of our hands. God keeps every promise to restore our lives.

Prayer:
Heavenly Father, I bless and honor You. I give You the highest praise. You are the Miracle Maker. Thank You for blessing me with Your amazing love and grace. Thank You for Your generous heart and all the gifts You've given me. Thank You for Your compassion and kindness. Thank You for healing my broken heart and restoring health to me. Thank You for all the wonderful benefits You bestow on me daily. Thank You for understanding me. Thank You for being close to me and saving me. Thank You for Your kindness to bring an end to my suffering through Your grace. Thank You for imparting Your blessing and favor. I ask that Christ Himself will perfect, confirm, strengthen, establish, complete me, and make me what I ought to be. Thank You for being my Teacher, my Helper, my Healer, my Redeemer, my Provider, my Good Shepherd, my Vindication, my Restoration, my Hope, my Salvation, my Prince of Peace and my Love. Thank You for Your unfailing love. Thank You for filling me with Your love, peace, and joy. Thank You for healthy, loving relationships. Thank You for a future that is bright and filled with promise. Thank You for success and the fulfillment of divine destiny. Thank You for